Childish Things

The Reminiscence of Susan Baker Blunt

August 1st 1918

In Compliance with the request of my youngest Brother Elbridge and his Wife, I will relate Some of the Events that occured in my Childhood as I remember them after the lapse of over Eighty years they seem very real to me as they are recalled to my mind

I was born on May fiftienth 1828 I was the forth Child, and my Mother was 21 and my Father 28 years old, it was fashimable in those days to marry very young. we lived in a Small country vilage called Thorntons Ferry; in the town of Merrimack, Hillsboro Co, New hampshire, it was bordered on the east, by the beautifull Merrimack river the vilage consisted of about ten houses with a large old tavern in the center; two Lawers Offices, a general Merchandice Store; and a large boarding house for the river Men; as all the transportion of goods at that time was by Cannell Boats and Rafts built of logs in the winter they used great wagons Covered with Canvass; and drawn by a number of horses, which they would Change at the large Stable, by the Tavern; Somtimes Father would work all night Shoeing horses; So they would be ready for an Early Start the next morning;

Page one of the Susan Baker Blunt manuscript. *From the Manchester Historic Association Photo Archives.*

Childish Things

The Reminiscence of Susan Baker Blunt

edited by

FRANCIS MASON, PH.D.

for

The Manchester Historic Association

Tompson & Rutter Inc
Grantham, New Hampshire
1988

© 1988 by the Manchester Historic Association
Notes and preface © 1988 by Francis Mason
All rights reserved
Printed in the United States of America
Published 1988 by Tompson & Rutter Inc, Grantham, NH 03753-0297

Library of Congress

Library of Congress Cataloging-in-Publication Data

Blunt, Susan Baker, 1828-1924.
 Childish things : the reminiscence of Susan Baker Blunt / edited by Francis Mason.
  p. cm.
 Bibliography: p.
 Includes index.
 ISBN 0-936988-14-2 : $8.95
 1. Blunt, Susan Baker, 1828-1924—Childhood and youth. 2. New England—Biography. 3. New England—Social life and customs.
I. Mason, Francis, 1935-   . II. Title.
CT275.B57985A3 1988
974!.03'0924—dc19
[B]   88-19027
                                               CIP

Contents

Foreword *by George Comtois* / 7
Preface / 9
Reminiscence of Susan Baker Blunt / 15
Appendix / 80
Bibliographic References / 81
Index / 85

ILLUSTRATIONS

First page of the Susan Baker Blunt manuscript / *frontispiece*

Susan Baker Blunt at age eighty / 14

Canal boats / 17

Stage coach in the days of the Mammoth Road / 19

Old Town Hall / 48

Province House, Boston / 56

Boston Museum / 59

First High School, corner of Derne and Temple Streets, Boston / 61

First Baptist Church, Boston / 65

Granite bridge, built in 1840—Concord Railroad, opened in 1842 / 72

Amoskeag machine shop ca. 1850 / 74

Susan Baker Blunt at age thirty / 78

Foreword

A slight mist through which objects are faintly visible has the effect of expanding even ordinary streams, by a singular mirage, into arms of the sea or inland lakes.—HENRY DAVID THOREAU in "A Week on the Concord and Merrimack Rivers" 1849.

Susan Baker Blunt, whose memoirs these are, was born on May 15, 1828, in the tiny river village of Thornton's Ferry in the township of Merrimack, New Hampshire. She was the fourth child of Robert Baker and Margaret Patten. She lived for ninety-five years, passing away near Los Angeles, California, in 1924, but not before she had recorded some of her more touching and informative memories of growing up along the banks of the Merrimack during the first half of the nineteenth century. These were the good and not-so-good old days before the Civil War, before Thoreau, with his brother, paddled past her village and penned the lines above, when "King" Andrew Jackson reigned over the United States and barge men ran the river.

This is not the diary of a young girl but the reminiscence of an elderly woman with a sharp mind and a good memory. It was written by the eighty-five year old Mrs. Blunt in 1913 at the urging of her younger brother Elbridge, who, no doubt, loved to hear his sister tell of her childhood in the little village of Thornton's Ferry.

It is not surprising that he enjoyed her stories so much, as you will find for yourself: she was a wonderful raconteur with a gift for making extraordinary the otherwise ordinary events of small town life in early rural America.

If you have a penchant for the past and find pleasure in it, then you have chosen the right book. For some time now, The Manchester Historic Association has wanted to see this manuscript published, since it came to us in 1968 from Miss Hazel Kimball, a grandniece of Mrs. Blunt. The manuscript has been thoroughly and expertly annotated by Dr. Francis Mason, whose purpose was to authenticate dates, places, and events, while clarifying what would otherwise be obscure or confusing references. Dr. Mason is a trustee emeritus of the MHA and a professor of history at St. Anselm College in Manchester, New Hampshire.

GEORGE COMTOIS,
Director, Manchester Historic Association

Preface

This memoir, the original of which is located in the archives of the Manchester Historic Association and is usually referred to as the "Susan Blunt Journal," was written by Susan Baker Blunt in 1913, when she was already eighty-five years old. It is her only known written reminiscence, though she never tired of telling stories of her past. Several years after composing this account of her young life in New Hampshire, Susan was still entertaining acquaintances with her stories. In 1920 she lived near Los Angeles with her younger brother who had originally encouraged her to record her childhood. She told her stories to women of the So Ever Club, a group of women who had worked together in the Red Cross.[1] This written record is Blunt's account of her childhood from 1818 to 1843, when she turned fifteen and became a "young woman and [was] done with childish things."

Susan Blunt's manuscript emerges as a fragment of a childhood, for it is no regular diary or journal. As literature the work suffers, but it is not as literature that the memoir holds our interest. Its importance lies in the historic value. Susan's childhood was not terribly extraordinary, but her story is delightful because she was an insightful and sensitive youngster and remembered well her past. She observes rural New Hampshire just as industrialization arrives on the scene. This rural setting is nicely juxtaposed with her one exciting school year in the bustling city of Boston. She reveals for us her "simple naritive," but she also makes considerably richer the period within these narrow geographical confines during the years 1828 to 1843.

Susan's memoir has wide appeal, even if her childhood was more typical than not. Taken totally, Mrs. Blunt's memoir will enrich the early American national period. She tells us of some of the last Indians still to roam the eastern countryside and of the first Irish immigrants to pass through New Hampshire. Susan will reaffirm many concepts about school conditions and reawaken our attention to the unsubtle rebellious nature of students. Her memoir will present some fine examples of children being used as help outside the rural family home. And Susan's words will remind us that rural life had its depressing moments. Early nineteenth-century New Hampshire rural areas had their share of suicides and a large number of mentally ill people, if the small community of Merrimack is any example. Nowhere is it likely that a more unusual story of the introduction of the tomato to American life will be found than here in Susan's account. Many other stories add to the charm as well as to the value of the work, ranging from the family's first kitchen cooking stove to the children's revenge on the railroad. Social historians seeking to uncover attitudes of those first factory workers moving from the farm to mill will appreciate Susan's memoir, but they may be disappointed that she did not contribute more on the subject. Still, her brief remarks about early mill life in Manchester may contribute in a small way to the discussion among historians of whether or not industrialization aided the liberation of women.

One particular matter should be noted about Susan's personal life. Genealogies indicate that she was married twice, first to Thomas Adams and then to Phineas Blunt. No dates are given for either marriage and there is no recording of children to either marriage. Phineas Blunt, however, was also the name of the uncle with whom she resided when she visited Boston as a young girl. Did she later marry this uncle? Did she possibly marry his son? I simply have not been able to answer the problem. Mr. Blunt and Susan's aunt had perhaps five children, but genealogies name only four of the children, and Phineas is not one of the four names. Thus one is left with the idea that she did marry her aunt's husband, or perhaps the genealogies are confused with the first names. There are two pictures of Phineas Blunt on file in the Manchester Historic Association, taken probably in the 1870s and 1890s, the latter photographed in San Francisco. Are these pictures of a son? Correspondence with living descendants has not clarified the matter. Nothing was learned regarding Susan's first husband.

Susan wrote the memoir in pencil in the remains of an account book. Essentially, there were neither sentences nor paragraphs in the original. Punctuation was seldom used correctly, but commas were Susan's favorite punctuation device. I chose not to follow the interesting format of Daniel Roche who edited the journal of a French eighteenth-century glazier as he wrote it, essentially without punctuation.[2] From a practical point of view, Mrs. Blunt's punctuation has been ignored in editing her memoir. All the sentences and paragraphs have been determined by the editor. Except for punctuation, the original narrative remains largely as it was first written. Only in a few instances has a word been omitted to facilitate an easier reading, and all such omissions have been marked with ellipses. Occasionally it was necessary to add words to clarify the meaning; these will be found in brackets within the text. Susan's spelling, including possessives, has always been retained. Whenever a word might be questioned, the correct spelling has been added in brackets. Some judgment has been made about retaining the original capitalization, since Susan did not always make clear her intent of certain letters. Finally, all words which she inadvertently repeated have been removed without notation.

The decision to edit the memoir has been dictated by several considerations. First the notes should clarify unusual references. They should also in some instances place the memoir in a larger historical perspective. But perhaps most importantly, the notes seek to prove the accuracy of Susan's memory. A memoir written at age eighty-five, even if it was a written account of stories frequently told, could be questioned as inaccurate or distorted. Such questions would lessen the historic value of Susan Blunt's memoir. Was Susan, for instance, tempted to elaborate her account to satisfy her listeners? John Neuenschwander has shown such distorting has occurred in the past.[3] Additionally her written account and a few known letters composed even after the memoir, give no evidence that Susan Blunt suffered from any of the psychopathologies often associated with elder citizens.[4] Research of her stories indicates, on the contrary, the accuracy of Susan's memory. This helps to confirm that many elderly recall their youth with surprising accuracy.[5] Perhaps even, as modern medicine and studies of the elderly conclude, being convinced finally at eighty-five to write down her stories may have helped Susan face more easily her remaining years of life.[6] In the final analysis Susan Blunt's memoir is of considerably more value because we know her memory can be trusted. Susan lived to be ninety-five, dying in January 1924 in West Covina, California.[7]

A list of Susan's family has been included at the end of the memoir as an appendix. This can be profitably used to check names when Susan sometimes refers to her brothers and sisters by order of birth rather than by name.

F.M.

Publisher's note: Dr. Mason's comments on Susan Blunt's reminiscence are printed in italic throughout her text. Numbers within parentheses refer to the listing in the bibliographical references found at the end of the book.

1. Copy of a letter to Hazel Kimball, a greatniece, 17 May 1920, Manchester Historic Association.
2. Daniel Roche, *Journal of My Life, Jacques-Louis Menetra* (New York, 1986).
3. See his "Remembrance of Things Past: Oral Historians and Long-Term Memory," *Oral History Review* (1978), particularly pages 45-53.
4. See T. L. Brink, "Oral History and Geriatric Mental Health: Distortions of Testimony Produced by Psychopathology," *Oral History Review* (1985), 93-105.
5. See Rob Rosenthal's thoughtful article, "The Interview and Beyond: Some Methodological Questions for Oral Historians," The *Public Historian* (1979), 58-67.
6. See particularly, Louise Tilly, "Individual Lives and Family Strategies in the French Proletariat," *Journal of Family History* 4(Summer 1979) 140 n.4.
7. A copy of her death certificate is in the collection of the Manchester Historic Association.

Susan Baker Blunt at age eighty. *From the Manchester Historic Association Photo Archives.*

AUGUST 1st 1913

In Compliance with the request of my youngest brother Elbridge and his Wife, I will relate some of the events that occured in my Childhood. As I remember them after the lapse of over Eighty years, they seem very real to me as they are recalled to my mind.

I was born on May fifteenth 1828. I was the forth Child, and my Mother was 21 and my Father 28 years old. It was fashionable in those days to mary very young. *[Susan's mother was Margaret Patten, a granddaughter of Matthew Patten of Bedford; her father was Robert Baker of Derryfield, Manchester's first name. Susan's mother certainly married young, evidently at about fifteen, though the genealogy is not definite. Her father would have been about twenty-two. Susan's observation that people married young in "those days" should not be treated as anything more than a statement about her own parents' marriage at an early age. Dates of marriage for her mother's brothers and sisters are not given in genealogies, but the evidence indicates that they did not marry as young as Margaret Patten Baker. Susan is also ignoring here the fact that three of her mother's five brothers never married, though all were at risk to do so.*

Demographic studies of New Hampshire and New England for this period are few, but studies made on colonial Massachusetts in particular have gone far to refute the old idea that marriage at an early age was the rule in the seventeenth and eighteenth centuries. Marriage by the 1820s probably was not being made at any significantly younger age either. A study underway by Joseph F. Kett and Peter Knights on the Sons of New Hampshire, covering the mid-nineteenth century, indicates that these New Hampshire men generally married between twenty-five and thirty.(1)] We lived in a small country village called Thorntons Ferry in the town of Merrimack, Hillsboro Co, New hampshire. It was bordered on the east by the beautifull Merrimack river. The vilage consisted of about ten houses with a large old tavern in the center; two Lawers Offices; a general Merchandice Store; and a large boarding house for the river Men, as all the transportion of goods at that time was by Cannell Boats and Rafts buildt of logs. In the winter they used great wagons covred with canvas and drawn by a number of horses, which they would change at the large Stable by the Tavern. Sometimes Father would work all night shoeing horses so they would be ready for an early start the next morning. The Tavern was well patronised by the Teamsters on there way from Vermont and northern NH to Boston with all kinds of produce: Beef and Hogs dressed for the market, great tubs of Butter, Lard and all kinds of Poultry and diary products. There was a Bar Room in the Tavern as well as in the large river Boarding house. And Rum was sold in the Store in any quantity to suit the custimers. In the Summer, when the Boats and Rafts were plying up and down the river, we could hear them blow a horn when they were a mile away. They would blow one blast to let the Landlady know they were coming and one blast for every Man on board,

WITH WIND AND CURRENT.

BOAT ENTERING LOCKS

MOVING UP THE RIVER

Canal boats. From Drawings by Henry W. Herrick. *From the Manchester Historic Association Photo Archives.*

so she would know how many to cook supper or dinner for. So by the time they landed there meals would be ready.

The first recollection I have of my self I was standing in a lane that went from the main road to the River. My Father stood by my side, smiling; and in front of me were two women, who had hold of my hands and were stooping down and looking in my Face as though I was some kind of a curiosity. I had run away from home, and my Father had just found me. I suppose I was lonesome as the Children had all gone to school, and I was trying to find them. The Man in the store would give me Candy, and that would attract me there; and I loved to go to the stable among the horses. I was not afraid of them, but my Mother was so worried for fier I would be killed in some of my wanderings, that she sent me to school with the rest of the Children. So at the age of three I Commenced my Education and have not finished it yet.

The next peice of mischeif I remember was going into the bedroom with a pair of sissors, . . . cutting off all my hair, and then going out and telling my Mother that I thought I would cut it off a little, just enougth to keep it out of my eyes. Mother sat down and cried she felt so badly, for I had long curls and I had spoiled my good looks. Not long after this she was not at breakfast table and I went to find her. She was in bed in the Spare room and a strange woman sat by the fire with a little baby in her arms. I walked up to her and took hold of its head with both hands. Mother spoke from the bed and said: "You must be very carefull and not hurt your little Brother."

When I was four years old I had my first real trouble. I used to go to one of the neighbors to play with a little Boy near my age. His Mother was very near sighted and hard of hearing. She would bring out great slices of bread

Stage coach in the days of the Mammoth Road. *From the Manchester Historic Association Photo Archives.*

and butter, but I never could eat mine. It tasted so strong of salt it made my mouth smart, so I would throw it away through a crack in the board fence. One day I found a cent in the road near the house. I caried it in and held it for her to take if it belonged to her. But she took no notice, so I thought it did not belong to her and caried it home. In a few minutes she came in and said I had stolen her little Boys cent. Mother was teribly shocked to think I would steal, so she gave me a very severe whiping and then told me she expected the shereff would come after me when he heard of it. So I crept off up stairs and hid where the shereff could not find me and went to sleep and so forgot my trouble.

Soon after this the [neighboring] Family moved away. When she got into the stage she forgot to put her Boy in, but she left him standing in the road. The driver started up his horses at full speed and the Boy ran on behind, schreaming "Ma, Ma," and she had her head out of the stage window Calling "Newton, Newton" at the top of her voice. Finely the driver understood the situation and took the Boy in.

I remember my first thanksgiving. My sister, on the day before, had told me to get up very earley in the morning to see old Thanksgiving go by. When I came down stares the next morning, they were all eating breakfast. Father looked up with a very sober face and said: "You are two late, Old Thanksgiving has gone by. His legs were so long they reached accrost the road, from one field to another. Next year you must get up earlier."

[It has not been possible to find a satisfactory source suggesting such a personification of Thanksgiving, and it may only have been a local phenomenon. But there is evidence that such a development would not have been out of place. Thanksgiving did not become a national holiday until during the Civil War. It had previously been celebrated in various ways in New England, frequently and originally, as a day of recreation. In some areas a custom developed to knock on doors of those people well-off, asking for gifts. Children were often dressed in costumes when requesting gifts. Though none of these aspects, similar to Halloween, are suggested by Susan, there is still in her narrative a sense of fun and teasing.(2)]

One day at school there was a great excitement. We could see men comeing down the road, carring guns. Every little while they would stop and shoot into the air and then hurry on again. If the Teacher had let us out, we could have seen Jeneral Jackson go by. But she let the large ones go to the windows, and the small ones could not get near enough to see him. I was so disappointed that I cried when I got home and told my Mother. There happned to be a carrage passing the house gust then whith two Men in it, and she said he looked like that Man; and I was satisfied. The President was on his way from Boston to Concord.

[Susan, now just past five, is recalling President Andrew Jackson's visit to New Hampshire at the end of

June 1833. The president was accompanied to New Hampshire by the vice-president, Martin van Buren, and they were met at the Massachusetts state line by officials of the state of New Hampshire. President Jackson did pass through Merrimack as his route from Lowell followed the river to Concord. And the president rode in style, the state having provided him with an open white barouche, drawn by four gray horses.(3)]

Sometimes a Circus would pass in the night with a Carivan of Animils and, for fier some one would get a free sight, they would travel after dark. One night when the Boys heard they were coming, they colected all the Shaveings they could find and strewed them all along beside the road. And when the Eliphants and Camels went by, they for once had a free show. One day a man came along with a show and stoped at the Tavern. He had a great Box looking waggon, with a door in the rear and steps to enter. I went in with Mother. On each side of the little room were little peices of glass which we looked through and could see pictures. And on a shelf accrost the front end, little wooden Puppets would come out and dance. It was a very hot day, and the Man used the door for a Fan.

At that time there were a great many Fish caught in the river through the months of May and June, when the Fish were on there way from the Ocean to Lake Winepasawque to lay there spawn. They used a big net with sinkers which they would tow out into the middle of the river, and then the Men in Boats would haul it in. Sometimes it would come in full and sometimes it would be empty, and then they would call it a blind hawl. They caught Shad Salmon and lamprey Eels, which they caught in an Eell Pot which was made of wooden slats at one end. The slats were inverted and built into the Box with a hole large enough for and [an] Eell to go through. Once inside they could not get out, and they would catch them by the thousand at Amoskeag Falls where they went over the great rocks. But when the big Dam was built at Lawrence it put an end to the fishing.

[The coming of the industrial plants destroyed the fishing industry along the banks of the Merrimack, but the dam at Lawrence was only partially to blame. Dams also at Lowell and Bow, New Hampshire, "checked completely" the passage of fish on the river.(4)]

One year there was a tribe of Penobscot Indians came up the river in there birch bark canoes and landed on the beach and pitched there tents. There were a number of Families, and they all had seperate tents. The Cheefs tent was much larger than the rest, and he and his wife both wore breast plates made of silver, as large as a tea plate. There were a number of Children, and they could all swim like ducks. The Mothers would carry the little babies to the river and throw them in and they would swim with the other Children as natural as life. On Sundays the tents were all cloased and they held meetings in the big tent, but on week days the Beach was thronged with visitors. The women made beautifull bead work and baskets. Some of the girls wore aprons made intirely of small beads of beautifull Colours, made like the bags that are used now. Some of the Boys were rougeish. One of them went into Father's Shop and stole a nice, new steel trap. Some one saw him and told Father, and he went for it. The Boy denied knowing any thing about it. Then Father went to the Chief and told him if it [were] not brought back, every tent on the Beach would be pulled down. Then the Boy brought [the trap] along with a dead rat in it, but Father made him take it to the river and clean it thourely. They stayed there a number of weeks and were very orderly, but the next year we were sorry to hear of there being all drowned in going over some Falls.

The next Spring we had another addition to our Family, a very pretty little Boy. His eyes and hair were as black as coal and his hair curled all over his head in little tight rings. He was very active and walked when he was nine months old. One day Father brought home a pair of heavy shoes and put them on his feet and stood him upon the Floor, when to our great surprise he ran accrost the great kitchen floor. After that he ran instead of walking.

At that time we had a pet Racoon who was very tame and cunning [and] would do lots of tricks. [He] would stand on his hind legs and drink out of a cup held in his fore paws. The little Boy and he would play on the floor like kittens. When the baby was eating, the Coon would try to take it away. [The raccoon] would run his paw into his mouth but would never bite or hurt him in any way, but it was fun for us Children to see them roll over and over. One day our next door neighbor made cup custerds and put them on a high shilf in her cupboard and shut the door and butoned it very carefully, but when she went to get them for the table she found the inside of each one scraped out [by the raccoon] with his paw. But he lift his tracks, so she knew who the rogue was who did the mischeif. One morning he attacked one of the little girls on her way to school and took her dinner basket away, so Mother had to give her another dinner to carry to school. Soon after this Father sold him.

This summer we moved into a larger house. It was very old [and] was built for a tavern in the colodion [colonial] days. It was well preserved as it had been taken good care of by the owner. The Parlor was a large square room with windows on three sides. One side was all taken up with a great fire place, with only room on each side for a door. There were Corner Cupboards; and the walls were wainscoated from the floor to the cealing, in panels and filergree work, and all painted dark green. There were two large rooms up stairs. One was finished off nicily where the Lady travelers slept, and the other was unfinished for the men when they put up for the night. In one corner of the front yard was a great rock that I injoyed very much by climbing up on it. I found a nice seat with a back where I would play by the hour.

The people in the vilage were very freandly, nice neighbors. They had parties sometimes in the winter. They would all go sleigh rideing in a big double sleigh with four or five seats and a span of horses with a cluster of sleigh bells on the neck of each horse. They would call at the door for Mother, and we Children thought it was something grand to see her go off in such stile. After the sleigh ride, they would go to some tavern for supper and in the evening have a dance in the hall. Every tavern had a hall where they could give dances. But we were never left alone at night, [for] Mother would have a woman come and stay all night.

There was quite an interval beside the river with a hard sandy beach where, on the 17 of June and the fourth of July, they would all assemble to celibrate the day by a dinner under the trees. *[June 17 is, of course, the anniversary of the Battle of Bunker Hill and was locally celebrated at this time in Merrimack.]* There were two rows of beautifull old Elms that reached the whole length of the beach. They would build a long table. There was a military company and a band of music to entertain. Down the center of the table there would be a long row of roast Pigs with a lemon in there mouths and a rose on its tail. The side dishes were numerous and of great variety. One summer one of the Ladies presented a new flag to the military Company and made an address and the Captain responded, but I was two small to remember much about it.

One of the days that we Children injoyed was the May training. I believe all the young Men in Town belonged to the Company, *[The men serving in the militia from Merrimack would probably have been a part of the Fifth Regiment. Some of the other New Hampshire towns represented in this regiment included Milford, Nashua, Hollis, and Hudson. The Fifth Regiment was a part of the First Brigade and the First Division.(5)]* and they would march around and make quite a display. But when they would halt before our house and give a Salute, I would run down [to the] celer, for I was affraid of the guns. After dinner at the tavern, they would go on a little hill in the rear of the village and have a sham battle. They had a small cannon which they would fire off, and it would attract many spectators and among them some very quear charectors.

I remember one in particlar, because he used to come to our house and talk to the Children. He would go to the Store and buy nuts and then come and borrow a hammer and treat us children. While we were eating he would point his finger at us and say, "you will die after you eat that," and then laugh as though he thought it was a great joke. When he was a Child he was very bright, but one day he followed his Father on the top of a high building where he was at work and fell off and injured his head so badly that he never recovered. He went by the name of Fool Peabody. There was another foolish fellow in the same place, and every time they met there would be a fight. When any one would ask Peabody why he hated Parsons he would say, "I am a Fool and I know it but he is a darned fool and don't know it."

There was an old Colered woman in Town that everyone called Aunt Jenny. She was a slave when young, as some of the people owned slaves in New England in the early days. She was very old and all the neighbors were very kind to her. I never knew in what part of the Town she had her home or we should have gone to see her, for we were all very fond of her.

[In 1820 there were nine free blacks living in Merrimack. Three, only one a woman, were over forty-five years old. The census did not give names, except for the head of the house. Most of the nine blacks were a part of the Cicero Sweat household. This does not identify Susan's "Aunt Jenny," but it does indicate that free blacks were not unique in Merrimack at this time.(6)]

My Brother, who was next older than myself, [and I] used to take long walks together and, when we were tiard, we would call at some of the farm houses and rest. We knew many of the farmers by there comeing to the blacksmiths shop to have work done. I remember one house where we used to call. It was so very clean the chairs, table, floor, and all the wood work was unpainted and was kept white by being scoured with sand. On the top shelf of the old fashioned dresser, that was built [along?] and nearly covered on [one] side of the kitchen, was displayed a row of pewter platers. In the center was a large one that was used when the family had a boiled dinner. In the center they would place a great peice of corned beef, another of pork, and all around the edges would be placed all the vegitables. They would always have a bag of beans boiled at the same time as a side dish. Clinton and I would set on one of the chairs with our little feet curled up on one of the slats for fier of soiling the white floor and, after we had drank a cup of butter milk, we would start on.

There was a Pond not far from our home called horse shoe Pond from its shape. *[The pond is still named Horseshoe Pond.]* There was a Penensulir in the center of the pond and a neck of land that led to it where we loved to go curiosity seeking. One day we found a large turtle and draged it home by puting a stick in its mouth. It snaped at it and never let go until we got home. Father was very fond of wild meat and thought we had a prise. So he cut his head off and dressed it and said there were four kinds of meat. It was full of Eggs about half as large as a hen's egg [though] soft shelled. But the outside skin was very tough, and we played ball with them for a long time.

My sister was six years older than I was. She was very lively and full of fun and was our ring leader in all plays, and we were now capible of geting up a Circus at most any time. One of our neighbors who lived accrost the street was very fond of Children, and they would call us over sometimes and give us a treat of something nice to eat. And then they would set in the window and watch us play on there lawn and laugh at our antic. They were all maiden Ladies but one, and she was a widow. We thought they were pretty nice. My oldest Brother wanted to give them a present so he made them a puding stick out of a shingle, to there great amusement.

He was [also] very fond of animels. When he was nine, he had a present of a calf and he wanted to raise it. But there was no place to keep it so they sold it to the Butcher. When he came for it, they could not find it for a longtime. At last they went up onto the highest scaffld and found it, where the Boy had draged it by a rope.

The Brother who was two years older than I was loved to work with tools. There was a carpenter's shop near the house, and the man would let him go there and use his tools and paint. And he used to make very pretty cradles and bedsteds, for my rag-babies. When he was nine he made a knife box for his Mother that is in use now among some of the grand-children.

About this time Father bought a new house with an acre of ground and a large front yard, which we all injoyed very much for a play ground.

At about this time the City of Lowell was pland, and the Company imported labourors from Ireland to dig Canalls to carry the water power to run the great Cotton Factories they were building. *[Susan understood correctly the expectations for the earliest use of Irish immigrants. One consideration for the establishment of cotton textile industries in New England had been a ready labor supply available on marginal farms in the region. Thus, the Irish were first imported not to work in the mills but to be used in the heavy construction work of mill building and canal digging.(7)]* For some reason they could not land them in Boston but they were landed in Quebeck. And then they travled down through the Country in great droves of Men, women, and children with great packs on there backs. They were very indipendent and aggressive [and] said they were in a free country and were ready for a fight any time. One day Father was at home diging potatoes. He had just dug up a bad one and threw it into the road without looking. There happned to be a tribe going by the house at that moment. One of the Men picked up the potato and came to the fence and said: "Did you throw this at my Child? If it had hit [the child], it would have been killed. Ile knock your two bloody eyes into one," and [he] treed [tried] to climb over the fence. But Father kept him off by raping [rapping] his fingers with the hoe. Then more Men came to the fence to help whip Father. [But] when Mother handed his gun out of the window and he pointed it at them, . . . they all scampered off as fast as they could until they were out of sight. One day a man called at the shop and wanted work and said he was from Irland. Father asked him if he knew and [any]

Bakers there. He said, "Oh yes, there is Lord Baker and Earl Baker and indeed all the big bug's names in Ireland is named Baker."

Father was a very benevolent Man. I never knew him to turn any one away who wanted a nights lodging or a meal [or] who were to poor to pay for it at the tavern. I remember two young women who were walking from Charles Town to Montreal soon after the Convent was burned in Charlestown. They were Nuns and were going to enter a Convent as soon as they reached Montreal. It was in the early spring and the roads were very muddy, and there shoes and the bottom of there dresses were all wet and muddy. They looked very young as they sat before the fire in the Evening drying there shoes. After breakfast they started on there long tramp. *[Here is a fine example of the accuracy of Susan's memory. In August 1834 the Ursuline Convent in Charlestown, Massachusetts, was burned by a mob, convinced that nuns were being held against their will by the convent's superiors. It led to a major outburst of anti-Catholicism in the Boston area. Evidently this had little effect on Susan's family or its hospitality, despite the family being Protestant. Most of the nuns were returned to Quebec in October of 1834, though three remained in Boston to be available for the judicial proceedings which followed. These were joined by two sisters, returning from Quebec, in December. In May 1835, or the springtime as Susan points out, two made their way (or returned) to Quebec. I am indebted to Sister Marcelle Boucher, archivist for Les Archives des Ursulines de Quebec, for certain aid in reconstructing these facts. Apparently the travelling Ursulines did not always make their way to Montreal and then to Quebec by train and boat, escorted by "fine priests and ladies" as the Annals of the Ursuline convent suggests.(8)]*

Another time a Man came to see Father and stayed all night. The next day he was taken sick with a fever and Mother took care of him. He was there a number of weeks. And when he went away he gave her an old gun, and that was all she ever received. He had two Sisters in the village who were well fixed, but they did nothing for him.

Our school district was three miles long, and our house was a mile from the school house so we had to carry our Lunch and stay all day. Maney of the Children would not see each other between schools—which was only three months in the summer and the same in the winter. There were a number of large Boys in the winter, and they usualy celibrated the first day of school by haveing a fight betwen the "down roads" and the "up roads," as they called themselves, to see which side was the strongest. The side that beat was the Champion for the comeing year. Sometimes they would aggree in not liking the Master, and then one of the large Boys would climb up on top of the house and stop up the Chimney and smoke him out. *[The "smoking-out" of the teacher recalled by Susan is an interesting reversal of the usual American tradition of "barring-out" of the teacher. In the latter case, students would barricade themselves in the school and challenge the teacher to gain an entry.(9)]*

Some of the young Men who taught in the winter schools were very severe in there punishments and used very little judgment in adminestiring it, as being able to whip the big Boys [was] one of the qualifications for being a succesfull Teacher. One Master had a strap that he would put arround the neck of a Boy and then hang him to the wall, allowing his feet to just toutch the floor. One day at noon my oldest Brother came home sick. He said the Master made him stand all the forenoon with his toes on a crack in the floor and then reach over and put his fore finger on another crack. He stood in that position until he droped. He came home at noon and told his Father who was a very high temperd Man. He took his Boy back to school and walked in without any cerimony and had a talk with the Master that he remembered the rest of the term.

I only went to the Summer School until I was eight years old, and the first day the Master asked me if I would come early the next morning and sweep out the room. My sister heard him ask me, and she made so much fun of him that I heard no more about it.

The small children went to a little private school in the winter, where we were taught to read and spell and knit. The first thing a child learned was the Alphabet, [but] I don't remember when I learned mine. There were little stories and pictures in the spelling book I used until I was eight. We learned abreviations, definetions, and the multiplycation table out of the same spelling book. We all read a verse out of the New testtiment every morning twice around the school. And the last exersise at night was spelling out of a dictionary and giveing the defination of the word the older Pupels read out of an historical reader, which has gone out of exestance to my regret. When a child I always liked my teachers with one exception. She would whip the small Children unmercifuly. And we all disliked her so much that, on the last day, we all tore up and threw away the rewards of merit she had given us.

[Susan's recollection of the early school house in Merrimack is an excellent addition to the record of discipline and student defense reactions to discipline (certainly it was more than mischievousness or vandalism) in early nineteenth-century schools in America. Later, Susan will tell of a more orderly school room in Boston, but even there she will note student defense initiative against

discipline. It was considered good pedagogy in the nineteenth century for the teacher to assert absolute authority over the students.]

There was one Family in our neighborhood who went to Washington every winter. He was a Lawyer and went as a Senitor. *[This neighbor and friend was James Bounaparte (sic) Thornton. He was never a senator, but he was a member of the New Hampshire legislature and Speaker of the General Court in 1827 and 1830. He also served as a comptroller of the United States Treasury, and in 1836 he was charge d'affaires at the American consulate in Callao, Peru. Evidently he did not die in Peru; but died in 1838 shortly after his return to the United States. He was buried in Thornton's Ferry. (10)]* He was afterwords sent as a Minister to Peru and died there of the Colery. He was a great friend of Fathers and sent him some valuable presents. One was a very handsome gun (the stock was carved wood) and a knif with a number of blades. And last of all he brought him home some tomato seed or love apple as they were called then. He said they had them on the table where he boarded, and he liked them very much. We had them growing in our garden always after that, but it was three years before we could eat one. Mother prepared them in diferent ways. At last she made a pie which we could not eat, so she gave it to the Pigs and they refused to eat it. So we decided they were good for nothing. But Father would taste them every time he went in the garden, and the third year he liked them. They were small compared with what they are now, and the vines would stain and smeled disagreely [disagreeably].

[This is one of the most interesting stories in Susan's memoir. The tomato, one of the many products discovered in the New World, in this case South America, was quickly

adopted by inhabitants in the south of Europe but made only slight progress at being accepted elsewhere. North Americans were slow to see the tomato as other than a decorative plant. It apparently was first grown in America as a food in Virginia in 1781. Efforts by Italians to introduce it in Salem, Massachusetts, in 1802 failed. But by 1835 it was a quotable fruit in the Quincy Hall Market in Boston. The Baker family, therefore, was not alone in rejecting the tomato as a table commodity, but the Bakers were among the first people in New Hampshire with enough courage to attempt to eat it. Mrs. Baker may have been the only housewife who tried to bake a tomato pie!(11)]

That year we had a new cooking stove, the first one in town. And the neighbors said we would all be sick before Spring. It was very large. The back [burners] could all be taken off, in "rimmers" as they called them, so they could use diferent sised kittles. When they were all off they could use the big brass kittle which would hold a number of gallons. The oven and cooking utencils were all very large. The tea kittle, [which] would hold a waterpail full [and] was shaped like a pail, had a block tin top and a copper bottom. Mother was pleased with it. It was easier to cook [with] than [using] the fire place. In a year or two all the neighbors had one, after they saw that we came out all right in the Spring. But we children missed the brigt fire light in the evenings. With the big back log and fore stick and pine knots betwen, it made our great kitchen look very bright and cheerfull in the evenings. And we used to love to sit around on the hearth and tel stories or listning to some older person telling a story. And when company would come in, they would all take turns in singing a song or telling a story. One night my Father asked one of the little Boys to pass around the apples. He was a comical little Fellow. He set the dish of apples in the middle of the floor and walked around it. It made a laugh.

One of our neighbors was an old lady who lived alone. We were great friends. She had a Loom and wove cloth. She learned me how to fill the little quills for the Shutle on a little quill wheel. I used to help her make matches to light her pipe with or the fire when it was going out. She would take sticks of pine and split [them] up into little thin peices about four inches long and tie them up into little bunches and dip one end into a dish of hot sulpher then put them on the kitchen mantle for future use.

At that time there [were] no stoves used at bed time. They would carefully cover up the live coals with ashes, and it would keep until morning. Wood was cheep then and [there was] pleanty of it. We had matches that came in a little box with a folded peice of sand paper on top of the matches. And to light one you had to draw if [across] the sand paper. The first lucifer matches I ever saw was some Father brought home one night and scratched on his pants. *[Friction matches were developed in England about 1827 and were first produced by hand in the United States in 1836. Machines for making matches were patented in America in 1842, but not all functions of the making of a match were combined into one machine until 1883. Around the world, additional matches were made in the home just as Susan recalled.(12) Friction matches were common enough in Manchester in 1839, however, for the fire wardens to regulate against any person keeping such matches in any building whatever unless they were stored in a metal container or other noncombustible material. In fact the wardens forbade the carrying of any matches on the person.(13)]* It created a sensation with us children; we thought it one of the wanders of the world.

We used whale oil or candles for lights evenings. Mother had a very handsome Astrae [astral] Lamp that was a present from Friends in Washington. The glass was set in a metal frame with glass danglers around the frame. Some of the grand children have it now. *[This lamp remains in the family even today. The current owner is Miss Hazel Kimball of New York City, a granddaughter of Susan's younger sister, Frances Effie, born in 1845 after the memoir ends.(14)]* She also had some antque dishes that came from the white house after Jacksons aminestration. Mother used to dip candles in the fall, enough to last all winter. When a beef was killed in the fall, she would use all the tallow for candles. On the evening before we would help her prepare the wicks. The Boys would cut a lot of Rods and she would cut the wicks the length of a candle and then string them on the rods. In the morning she would comence her days work. She had an old fashioned chair, with a very long back, which she would turn down so the back would be right side up to hold the rods and put the big kittle of hot tallow at one end. And then [she would] seat her self so she could reach the rods easily and then dip each one in the hot tallow and straten out the wicks so the candles would be straight when they were finished. When she had gone over them once, she would commence again at the other end and so keep on until the candles were large enough. She kept the kittle full by turning in hot water. She also had candle moulds that she used when the diped ones were gone. She would tie in the wicks firmly and stick the small end into a potato, then fill the moulds with hot tallow ang [and] hang them up to harden.

I remember once an old Man came to our house and stayed all night. It [In] the evening, when he was reading the newspaper, he held the candle so close to the paper that he sat it on fire. He put the fire out and then asked my sister to take the scissors and cut out the burned edges so his wife would not see it. I don't know who he was as I never saw him before or afterwards.

One Cold winter morning I heard a low rap at the outside door. I opned it and a wild looking Man stood there shivering and half clothed. He rushed in passed me and went to the fire and sat down and began to talk. He said the children all loved him better than they did Jesus Christ and jumped up and danced around the room, and we saw a chain dangling from around his waist. One of the little Boys went to the shop for Father, and he came with two Men and took him away. He was a poor Crazy Man who had broken his chain and escaped. There was another Crazy Man in Town who was kept Chaned in a barn. His insanity was caused by over studying in the summer. When the big barn doors were opned any one could see him as they passed by. If they stoped to look at him, he would say "much learning makes me mad."

One day I was in a field alone picking wild violets. I happened to look up and a Man was looking into my eyes so wild that I was frightend and started for home on the run. He lived about a half mile from us and soon afterwords was taken violently insane, so that Father had to go and help take care of him until they could take him to Charlestown to a Lunitic Asylum. *[The New Hampshire Asylum for the Insane in Concord was not opened until 1843. Before that, insane persons who committed a crime were imprisoned as their only treatment.(15) Evidently there was neither state aid nor official concern unless the insane committed a crime. This may help to explain why families chained their mentally ill members.]* He resented haveing any one go to his house, and he asked Father if he had a rope. He told him that he had. "Then," he said,

"I wish you would go home and hang yourself." He was an old Bacheler and had a house keeper who went there to live when she was eighteen. They were now past middle life, and every body liked them and called them Uncle Billy and Aunt Easter. He got well in the Asylum, and when he came home they were married.

One day I was alone in the house takeing care of the Baby when I saw a Boy go by on a horse at full speed and whiping his horse at every step. In a short time he went back with the Docter on his own horse as fast as they could go to try and save his Father who had hanged himself. His wife found him in the barn. She was a small woman and he was a heavy Man, but she [had] lifted him up and held him while the Boy cut the rope and went for the Docter. But he was dead before they found him. He left a large family of children and a large Farm and he was a rich Man, but he became insane by brooding [over] the fier of comeing to want.

There was an old Lady who lived on the opposite side of the river who was very excintric. She owned a little house and lived alone. She would come over sometimes and call on the neighbors. She always carried a large work bag on her arm. One day Mother was frying doughnuts when she came in. She said she [was] in a hurry and could not stop long. She kept walking around the room, and every time she passed [the] Pan of doughnuts she would put one in her bag and say: "I never eat doughnuts Mrs. Baker." She came of a very nice family. Her Father was a judge and her Brothers were Lawyers in high standing, but they could not do any thing with her. She would tell them [that] one Man can lead a horse to water but twenty Men can not make him drink.

One of my Fathers young Sisters came to make us a visit with her intended; they came with a horse and shase [chaise]. He put the horse in the stable and came in to supper. Soon after a Boy came in and said the horse was sick. The young Man and Father went to the stable and were gone only a few minutes when someone raped at the door. Mother went to the door to see what was wanted and met three Men carrieing Father. She screamed and ran to him, but one of the Men pushed her out of there way and she sat down faint with fright. The horse had died of Colic and, in its strugles, had kicked Father on the Leg and broken two bones below the knee. That night my fifth Brother was born prematurely. We had a very capible hired girl and the Doctor and his wife were very kind as well as the rest of the neighbors. Father sold his blacksmiths shop at this time and became deputy shereff of the County.

When I was eight years old I had a present of a very nice wax doll, the only doll I ever had. But I had plenty of rad [rag] babies and played with them until I was twelve years old. But this doll was a wander; it had glass eyes and real hair. I kept it laid away very carefully in Mother's top draw [drawer]. One day I went to look at it and it was ruined. The sun had shone in so hot that it had melted the wax to my great greef. *[Most likely this doll was English made. Though wax dolls were handmade regularly in England and France as early as the eighteenth century, they do not seem to have been manufactured until the 1820s in England and not until after the Civil War in America. Dolls with eyes that closed were a part of doll making as early as 1810.(16)]* After this I made my own rag babies. I had a patern; it was a lot of work I thought. The last one I made I worked all day making the body and then hid it away until I could make its cloths. When I came down stars the next morning, my doll was suspended by the neck on a hook over the kitchen stove. The Brother next older than me had played a trick on me.

Mother looked so smiling and the rest were all laughing, so I could not get angry. But [I] felt a little asshamed and never made another.

We had one neighbor who was always calling for me to come over and take care of her cross baby. He was a dull, heavy child and was always crying and fussing, and I grew tiard of the imposition and would go and hide when I saw her comeing. But she would tease Mother until she would call me, when [then] I would go very reluctlatly. They were rich people but very stingy, and she never gave me any little thing that would please a child or even asked me to stay to lunche. I would go home for that and perhaps in an half hour she would come after me. Father asked me one night what she said. I told him she said "thank you." He said, "next time you tell her 'thank you' starved a cat once," but I never did. I have often wandered why they let me go there so much against my will, but I suppose they knew best.

I had a little cousen who was an orphan. Her Mother died when she was three years old and her Father deserted her and left her among strangers, but kind relitives found her and brought her home. She cam to our house when seven years old. She was very lively and entertaining [and] would tell us long stories about places where she had been liveing. She had a very vivid imageination, and I loved to hear her talk for I was naturaly a silent, quiet child. We both had some sewing and knitting work to do in the morning before we could play. She would get her stint done first, and then we would make the house lively for a while. She would go to the store and buy candy and have it charged to Father. My sister went to a singing school that winter, and, one day, my cousen told me we had been invited to go that night with one of the neighbors Boys who was to come for us. So we both dressed up in our white dresses and gause scarfs and sat around in state all the afternoon. I noticed that Mother and my Sister were laughing and haveing lots of fun together; but when she started for the Singing School and no one came for us, I began to understand the joke.

Our last little baby was now about twenty months old, but he could talk and sing every thing [that he] heard the rest of us sing. He learned every song they sung at the Singing School. He called himself Capt Bob. He was very small of his age and was never well until he was twelve, but he was possessed of a very merry happy disposition. He had white hair and great blue eyes [and] was very pale and thin. When he was tiard, he would say, "I want to go in my cradle house." There was a great contrast betwene the two youngest Boys: one was so very dark and the other so light, but they agreed well together all there lives. *[Susan is obviously referring here to the two youngest boys at the time: George W. (b.1835) and Robert Bradford (b.1837).]*

One day we had an invitation to go cranberring in a meddow some little ways from the house. It belonged to one of our farmer friends, who had gathered all they wanted and offered us all the rest of the crop for the picking. So my oldest Brother got a team that would carry quite a party, so we went. When we got to the house, he put the horse in the barn and [we] went on foot to the meddow. There was a small pond we had to cross or go around it. The two oldest went in a boat and sang sailor songs all the way accrost, but we got there first. And [we] were finding pleanty of cranberies when it began to rain, but we kept on picking until our pails were full. By that time we were thourly drenched, and we returned to the house driping wet. The Lady built up a big fire in the great fire place and had us all stand around the fire until our clothes were dry, and she gave each of us a cup of hot water to drink with a tea spoonfull of black pepper in each cup to prevent our taking cold. Then she went to work and prepared supper for us all. The table looked very pretty, I thought. She had taken out her best dishes that were all pink. At every plate she put a little cup plate about the size of a dollar to put our cups in when we poured out our tea into the saucer to drink. *[Cup plates seem to have been a particularly popular piece of tableware in America and evidently came into wide use with the development of the glass pressing machine about 1825. Cup plates were produced, however, in the early 1820s in England for the American market. Most of those made in America were produced in New England, orders dating from as early as 1827. These cup plates were sold all along the East coast. Drinking from saucers had been a common practice in eighteenth-century Europe while, in America, it was more usual to drink from the cup without any attempt to cool the liquid in a saucer. By 1800, however, the situation had reversed. Europeans considered it unfashionable to pour the liquid into a saucer while Americans began to adopt the custom. The cup plate must have been a refinement of the custom in American minds. By 1846 there were guidebooks for setting a proper table with cup plates.(17)]* She made hot buiscuit[s] and she gave us pleanty of honey, for they kept Bees. There were three kinds of pie and cake, which we all injoyed very much and went home feeling rather highlarious. The rain was over and we sang all the way home; we had such a good time.

When I was about ten a woman, who lived about a mile from us, came to see Mother. She wanted her to let me go and keep house for her for a week. She had two little girls and her aged Father to leive in my care. Mother let me go and told me to work like a little spider. The first morning the old man called me at five o'clock to get up and get his breakfast. I got up and went to the well after a pail of water; it was quite a distance from the house that I had to carry the water. Then I boiled some potatoes and fried pork and made coffee. I had to cook over a fire place, hang[ing] the kittles on hooks that were hung on a crane that would swing off the fire when the things were cooked. I set the coffee Pot on some coals on the hearth. After I had cleered away, I put on some beans to stew for dinner and had enough left over to last two or three days. Then I made some buiscuit[s] and baked them in a tin baker, set before the fire. The little girls went to school every day and I was alone, for the old Man slept most of the time. One day there came up a most terrific thunder shower and frightened me half to death, but the old Man slipted through it all. The woman came home at the end of a week and gave me a nine-pence for my weeks work, and I bought me a new calico apron.

When I came down stars one morning in April I found I had a new baby sister. I was glad it was a girl and very much pleased that I had a little sister. She was very pretty [and] had black hair an inch long. They had parted it in the middle, and the nurse said she had aught to have side combs. She had blue eyes and her skin was very white. They named her Margaret for Mother. I thought she was beautifull.

At about this time my oldest Brother and Sister left home. He went to work on a farn [farm] and my Sister kept house for him and a Bachelor Uncle, who was Father's partner in buying the farm. It was a portion of grand-Father Baker's property, who owned large tracts of land in Manchester NH. At the time of his death there were no debts on the property. But the admistrater, by the advice of a very sherwd Lawyer, kept selling off peices of land here and there at a very low price, as land was not concidered very valuable at that time; and he [father] had to raise money to pay the Lawyer for his advice. Father was not satisfied with the way the Estate was being settled, so he bought out the hiers and had a farm of seventy five acres. [He] built a large barn and house. . . . We did not move there for two years, but the two oldest children stayed [there] until the rest of the family came.

GrandFather Patten lived about nines miles from our house, and Mother used to drive there often to see her Mother who was a consumptive. She would put as many of us into the waggon and, with a baby in her arms, would drive there and spend the day. We had a young Uncle there who was three years younger than my sister. The Family were all gone except another Uncle who was a young Man. The housekeeper was another Uncle's widdow who had a little girl, so we had a good time there.

[Susan's grandfather was Alexander Patten, son of Matthew Patten of Bedford, New Hampshire. Matthew Patten was an important figure in the New Hampshire General Court in 1776 as well as serving as a member on the Committee of Public Safety. The uncles Susan refers to are not easy to identify. Twin uncles, born in 1825, would be three years younger than her sister Sophronia. Isaac never married, but for David to have been gone from home because of marriage at this date (even though Susan is indefinite as to the date, it was before 1841) would mean that he married very young indeed. The uncle who was a "young man" could have been either Greenleaf (b.1811) or James (b.1819), neither of whom married. The widow would have been Sally Hutchinson, wife of John Patten, the only uncle who married besides David; but David lived until after 1903.(18)]

Father owned a very fine horse and gigg which he used in his business as deputy shereff. One day, when Mother was on her way to visit her Mother, the horse got frightened at a butcher's Cart and ran away and threw Mother out and the two Children, but they were not hurt. The Baby was so well wraped up in mother's cloak that it escaped [harm]; the older Boy had some scratches on his face and that was all. The Man who drove the Butcher's Cart took care of them [and] caught the horse, and she came home all right. Not long after this Grandmother died and grandFather came to live with us.

The next winter my Brother came home from the farm and said Sophronia was very sick and the Dr said it [was] brain fever. So they hurred away that afternoon, takeing the baby and leiveing the rest of us to take care of ourselves. We got along all right. They were gone two weeks, and then I went to help take care of my sister. We went in the two wheeled gigg, and my Brother, next older, drove the horse. The seat was very broad and deep, and little Bob sat between us on the way. The wheels went over a rolling stone and I fell out, and the wheel went over both my legs but did not hurt me in the leist. The road was sandy and that saved me. We reached the farm all right and found my Sister able to be about the house. She gained strength fast and was soon able to help with the work. She was glad we brought little Bob, and he sang songs all the evening. Some of the girls came in to see us and we had a pleasant evening. There were a number of large families in the neighborhood. In the next house there were eight children. On the other side there were six, some of them were full grown. We had a family of cousens near by, so we were not lonesome for the want of company.

That Summer there was no school, only a little private school taught by a young girl. There was no school house in the district, but there was a large shoemaker's shop used for that purpose. But it was so far away for the small children to walk in the winter, that Father fitted up a small building he owned near by into a school room. And the next year he gave a house lot, and there was a nice school house built on it.

[This school, which Susan's father built, was the original school of Manchester's "suburban" District Three. It was, in other words, the origin of the Bakersville School of today. The school over the years received its share of praise and criticism in the annual reports of the School Committee. Eventually, however, the school could not provide the needs for the district's increasing population and, in 1853, fell into disrepair. The Baker family retained much interest in the school in the early years. Susan's father served as chairman of the Prudential Committee for 1844-45. Her older sister, Sophronia, was the summer teacher for 1846. By 1863 the building was described by the School Committee as catching up with the worst school in the city: "cold, dilapidated, disgraceful." In 1864, at a cost of little more than eighteen hundred dollars, a new school was erected for the district, making it "one of the most attractive school buildings in the city." This school was a forty by thirty foot structure. By 1881, the citizens of Bakersville were petitioning for a newer school building. Land was purchased, and a thousand dollars apparently was earned from the sale of the old building and its land. In 1883 a new Bakersville school, a brick building, was erected at the site of the present Bakersville school (built in 1917). Three full-time teachers were employed for teaching in 1883.(19)]

Mother had a lot of relitives, who lived on the oposite side of the river [and] who visited us sometimes. Among them were three maiden Aunts, who were quite old but were very nice and loviable. The oldest one was Aunt Polly who had a remarkable memory for dates. When the history of the Town was writen, she was a great help to them in giving them the corrict dates of the Town events. The other Aunts name was Sarah, whose whole life had been devoted to the care of the sick and helpless. In her youth she was ingaged to be married, but she broke the ingagement to take care of her Mother who was an invalid. After her Mothers death, her Brother had a parelitic shock and lived many years. Then Aunt Polly fell and broke her hip and was never able to leive her bed afterwords, but Aunt Sarah was able to wait on her and outlived her many years. *[These "aunts" were Susan's mother's aunts, Mary (Polly) and Sarah. Neither married. The third aunt, whom Susan does not name, probably was Jean, also unmarried. There is a footnote in the 1903 history of Bedford stating that both Polly and Sarah were interviewed for the writing of the town history in 1850. It is this history that Susan refers to.(20)]* They gave away there property to a man and his wife for takeing care of them. They were good, honest people, very releigeous, and took the best of care of the old Ladies.

One of my Mother's sisters came to our house to make a viset soon after we had moved to Manchester. My Sister and one of my Brothers and I went with her to visit the old Ladies. It was always a pleasure to viset them; they gave you such a hearty welcome. We went on Saturdy and stayed until monday, when we went on to the west paresh to viset cousens. Sunday morning they had family worship and such a prayer I never heard. He said, "Lord! can you tell me what it is that makes folks act so down here? Well I tell you Lord it [is] because they dont know any thing Lord. They dont know as much as my horse." It was a long prayer, and, when it was trough, my sister and I went out doors and ran for the orchard where we lay down under the trees and roled over and over to keep from laughing. She had a very mirthfull dispotion [disposition] [and] had laughing brown eye[s] that always expressed mirth.

When we moved to Manchester, a company of capilalests [capitalists] from Boston had bought the water priledge [privilege] and a large track of land that extended three miles back [from the river] and the same distance in the other diriction, had the Canals made and two large Cotton Factories in operation, [and] had laid out the City. There was a very long business street about a quarter of a mile from the river and ran parelell with it. The land on the west side [of the business street] was reserved for the erection of boarding houses for the operatives and smaller houses for the overseers. The streets were all laid out at right angles, and shade trees were planted on both sides of every street. They left open spaces every few blocks, that were laid out with walks with trees which added much to the beauty of the city. It was not incorperated as a city until 1849 [1846]. *[Early in 1838 the Amoskeag Company planned the first stages of the new city of Manchester. Surveys followed and the streets were laid out and house lots plotted. The principal thoroughfare was named Elm Street, though there were those who preferred to call it Broadway. Elm trees were planted along the street in the spring of 1839. Additional streets and squares to serve as parks were added and sites were even assigned for churches, schools, public buildings, and cemeteries. Six tenement blocks were erected by the company to help house the workers at the first mill, completed in 1839.(21)]*

We lived a mile below the City hall. There was a large cemitary on one side of the road, and a peice of woods

Old Town Hall, 1841-1844. From the Manchester Historic Association Photo Archives.

on the other. It made it very lonely and not always safe for a young girl to go alone. I was frightened once when on my way home from the city were I had been on an erend. I was almost through the woods when a Man overtook me and spoke. He asked me if my sister was at home [and] said he was going right down to my house. I thought he was an acquentance of Sophronia and was all right, until he asked me to go in the cemitary with him. Then I knew he was an imposter and hurried on as fast as I could until I came in sight of a house. When [then] he turned around and said, "I will give you five dollars if you will go back with me." I made him no reply but hurried on and he went back, and I never saw him again. When I got home Mother said, "What is the matter?" I said, "Nothing." She said, "Now I know there is and you tell me what it is." So I told her about the insult I had on my way home. She said, "He aught to have a good horsewhiping," and went out and told Father. And he went back and tried to find him but could not. I think he was a stranger going through the city. I was only twelve at that time but large of my age.

In the Fall and winter months the young people used to give little parties. One night we went to spend the evening at [our] nearest neighbors. Among other games, we played blind-mans bluff. It came my turn to be blind folded and I had almost caught a little girl, when she jumped onto [the] stone hearth and I after her with both arms out. But I caught hold of a boiler of hot water and pulled it over onto me, and it drenched me from my neck to my feet. They got my clothes off me as fast as they could and applied what remedies they had, then roled me up in quilts and drew me home. When I went into the house, Mother thought I was playing and looked up and smiled. I said, "Mother I am scaled [scalded] to death," and I thought

I was. The Dr lived a mile away, but they got him there in a very short time; and he applied lime water and linseed oil, and I was soon releived. *[Lime water and linseed oil were both common remedies for scalds at the time. However, it appears that usually something was added to keep the air off the burn, air being considered a dangerous element for burns. One remedy recommended the use of lime water on the scald before applying a wheat flour over the wound.(22) Another remedy suggested turpentine or linseed oil before applying flour.(23)]* I did not realise suffering so very much until it began to heal. The docter said there was danger my chin growing on to my shoulder, as my neck was swolen out even with my chin, which was drawn around and rested on my shoulder. But my Mother watched me day and night, and I owe it to her that I lived and was not deformed. I seemed to benumed or parilised. They would tell me to try and turn my head around, but I was not worried about any thing and thought if I was deformed it would be all right. But soon I got well, and in two weeks I was up and about the house.

One day not long after this, an Aunt and Uncle on my Fathers side came to make us a little viset. When they were ready to go home, they invited me to go home with them [and] said there was going to be a big country party it [in?] town and they thought I would injoy it. So with my Fathers consent I went, for I was always ready to go somewhere. It was quite a long drive but was interesting to me as I had never been in that part of the country before. We passed through a small manifactureing village where they made glass and there was a small cotton Factory; then we went through a long strate street for about four miles; then up a long hill to a place called the Borrough where they lived. *[The village most likely is

Suncook and the long street is Pembroke. The "borrough" remains unclear.] It was night [when] we got there, and I was tiard and homesick.

But the next day I was all right when the two young girls came to see me that I had never seen before. They were Cousens and I went home with them and had a fine time. It was the fashion then to try prodjects when a lot of young people met together. They would try tricks for fun to see who there future husband or wife would be. The one we tried that night was to take a looking glass in your hand and go down the celler stars backwards in the dark, then hold the looking glass before your face and say over, "My true love, whoever you be come and look in this glass with me." One of my cousens went down all right, and her Mother crept down after her with a mans hat on and a candle in her hand, lighted, and looked over her shoulder into the looking glass. But she knew her Mother and was not frightened. But the rest of us would not try it. Some old women believed in them and in witches and seeing ghoasts and would tell stories that would frighten any one, if they beleived the nonsence.

The next day we all went to the party. The house was quite large and the rooms were all full when we got there. They played games all evening, all joining hands and marching around and around the rooms singing and chooseing partners. It was all new to me, but I soon learned the games. When supper was ready we all marched out into the great kitchen and stood around a long table that was piled with plates and every thing else that was good to eat: piles of bread and butter, pans of doughnuts, pies, and cakes of all kinds, cheese and pickles but no meat. After supper they had dancing and more games until twelve o'clock, when we all went home.

On the East Side of our house accrost a small pasture

was a large growth of old pine trees. They were not very near together but spread over quite a large peice of ground. There was no under brush but there was grass and now and then a cluster breaks as they called them then. (They were large ferns that had been misnamed.) There was a cart road through the woods. About half way through was a spring of water that came up out of the ground. We called it our mineral spring, because where the water ran on the ground it looked like Iron rust. Beyond the woods was a grove of silver birches where my sister and I used to strool sometimes in the afternoons. We both loved the woods.

One day Father came in and told me one of the turkeys had stolen her nest and was sitting on the eggs and if I could find her I might have all the young turkeys. So the next time she came home to be fed I followed her. She went into the woods and I kept at a distance behind trees. Every little while she would stop and listen and look all around and then start on slowly again. At last she started and ran as hard as she could and then stoped and sat down. I marked the place and the next time she went home to eat, I went and counted the eggs. There were fourteen and she brought them all out in the Fall. I gave away two and sold twelve.

There was another field that joined our land called Swifts pasture that had a spring of Ice Cold water. We called it the boiling spring because we could see it bubling up through the sand at the bottom. We used to drink it out of cups made of leives when we were out berreing, and I have never drank water since that tasted as good as that did.

One summer the little Boy had the hooping cough, and our Family Dr happned to call and said he would give him something to releive him. And [he] left orders with my sister to give him a teaspoon full every half hour until it opperated. Mother was away somewhere that afternoon so Sophronia followed the Drs directions, but the effect was not satisfactory. She sent for Father. The Boy became unconcious and his stomach and bowels were swolen and as hard as a rock. Father went for an old Dr who lived on the other side of the river. He brought the old Dr and a jug of rum he had ordered. He said he had taken antimony enough to kill three Men and to toutch him up with rum. Mother came home at night, and they brought him out of danger but very weak. In the morning he wanted some water from the boiling spring, and they brought a ten quart pail full and set it by his bed. And he said no one could have a drink unless they paid him ten cents a glass. Little Capt Bob never forgot to joke, but he had no use for Dr after that night.

In the summer of 1841 they commenced building the railroad through from Nashua to Concord. While they were diging accrost our land down by the river, it was very hard for the workmen to find a place to board among the Farmers. They were all Country Boys; and, as Father never had two many in the House and Mother was always willing to work, they let some of them come there to board. They filled the little out house full of beds, and they stayed there three months. Mother had to work very hard with no help but us two girls, and I was not old enough to go ahead and take much care. Mother used a barrel of flour every week. One day a young woman called and wanted work and Mother hired her, but she proved to be not respetable and Mother sent her away.

In the mean time, one of Mothers sisters came to see us on her way to visit other Friends. On her return to Boston, where she lived, she came back to our house and insisted on my going home with her and staying a year and going to school. *[This aunt was Susannah who was married to Phineas Blunt.(24)]* They finally gave ther consent and I, child like, was willing to go. I think it must have been natural for me to travel, for I was always ready and willing to go. So they baught me some new clothes and I left home. We went in the stage as far as Nashua, when I saw the Steam Cars for the first time. The Car we rode in was very small compared with the ones that are used now. They were not up holstered but were painted and varnished and looked very new and nice to me. When we reached Boston, we rode in a hack to the house. And when we struck the Cobble Stones the streets were paved with, I thought the buildings were tumbling down, it made such a racket after being accustomed to sandy roads all my life. I was a little frightened and felt dizzy and confused. But after we came to the house and had supper I was all right until bed time, when I was homesick and cried myself to sleep.

The next morning my two little cousins escorted me to the Common, and I thought it was the most beautifull place I had ever seen. The trees were not very large then with the exception of one very large old elm, that was celibrated for its age by the Indians before Boston was settled. It was partly distroyed by lightning in 1860. *[This elm tree was long a favorite sight on the Boston Common. It was believed to have existed even before the settling of Boston in 1630, but by 1755 many considered it already "decrepit." Still, it must have been impressive at 72 feet in height and 22-1/2 feet in circumference. I found no confirmation of Susan's comment that it was partially destroyed by fire in 1860, but it was blown down in 1876.(25) The elm had also been used as a hanging tree. Mrs. Ann Hibbins was hanged in 1656 as a witch from the elm.(26)]* The greatest attraction then was the frog pond where the Boys could sail there boats. The lower part of the Common under the hill and next to the public garden was not improved, only a little border of flowers close to the fence on beacon street.

The house where we lived was nexd door to the old province house, where the old privincial Governor lived; and the court we lived [in] had been his garden. It was a very large old Mansion with an imposeing front that faced on Washington Street, where there was an Inn keepers sign on the door. There was a large yard all around it and an arch way that led to Washington St opposite the Old South Church. *[The "mansion" Susan describes was, of course, the Province House. Following the Revolutionary War, the former residence of the royal governor—which eventually was deeded to the Massachusetts General Hospital—was leased for various uses from "Orphic Minstrels" to drinking saloons. Susan's observation that it had a tavern sign in 1841 rings true. The gardens of this estate were gradually occupied with new buildings, constructed along the original driveway leading to the stables at the rear of the Province House. This passage was named Province House Court, and the Blunts lived at number 17. By the 1880s the buildings erected on the grounds could be referred to as "paltry," and the old Province House had been gutted by fire.(27)]* There was a large Ell that extended back into the Court. A Family of girls lived there that I liked very much. There were a number of girls who lived in the Court; and, after I was acquainted with them, I became more reconciled to my new home. The house we lived in was four stories with a large atic. On the first floor was a dining room and kitchen, on the next was a parlor and sitting room, on each upper floor were two sleeping rooms, [and] there was a celler where good wood was kept. Every body burned

Province House, Boston. *Courtesy of the Society for the Preservation of New England Antiquities.*

wood then. When a load of wood was brought into Court, a wood sawyer would follow with a saw and saw horse and fit it for the stove and pile in the celler. Ther was a big brick oven in the kitchen and every Saturday evening my Aunt would do her weeks baking. After she had taken out her bread, pies, and cake, she would put in a large pot of beans and another of pudding for the Sundays dinner. There was always room enough for one or two of the neighbors bean pots.

On the first Sunday afternoon we walked over to Bunker Hill to hear an address by a Mr Moffet. The Monument was only about half done then but was completed within a year or two afterwards. *[Though the beginning of the Bunker Hill monument project was celebrated in 1825, construction was not actually begun until 1827 and not completed until 1843.(28)]*

My aunt had a number of callers after she got home, and she introduced me as her little girl. I was not pleased for I was as tall as my Aunt. One woman said when she was introduced: "She is slim aint she for a Country girl?" I never liked the woman very well afterwards, although she was a constant visitor at the house.

The next week my Mothers other sister came in town for me to go home with her on a visit. *[This aunt was Hannah, the eldest child of Alexander Patten. Her husband, A. Coolidge, had died in 1830. Later she married again, a John Deavall.(29)]* She was a widow and lived with her husbands Mother on a large market farm, where they raised all kinds of vegitables and frute. They kept a lot of cows and sold the milk. They were rich people, had inhereted a large property, but were always reaching out for more money. When my Aunt introduced me she said, "Dont you think she is a pretty good sized thirteen year old girl?" One of them said, "I should think she was sixteen by her looks." At the end of the week the Aunt in Boston came after me and I went back to the city, but I had injoyed a very pleasent visit.

I could not drink the water in Boston, it was so brackish. It was not brought [piped?] into the city then and not for a number of years after. *[A public water supply was not, in fact, a part of the Boston scene until 1848. On 25 October of that year there was a huge celebration at the Frog Pond in the Common to commemorate the opening of a public water system piped into the city.(30)]* They had wells and used great wooden pumps. I had to resort to tea and coffee for the first time. We had breakfast at six. Every afternoon she [the aunt] would have lunch. She made every thing very rich [and] would have frute cake and mince pie for lunch with a boul of coffee, then have dinner at twelve and supper at six. But I dont remember of haveing indigestion. I took a bad cold when I first came to Boston, so I was not sent to school until the winter turm.

One of my Mothers young Brothers came to the house to board that winter, and he was very kind and thoughtfull of me. I went with him to all the Lycium Lectures and I heard an Organ for the first time. One evening he took me down through Fanuel hall and Quincy markets and bought some lobsters, the first I had ever seen. Every thing was new and strange to me. One day we went to the Musium. It was then on Sudbury Street and the Exibition was in a number of rooms. *[It is possible that this museum was the New England Museum which was located, not on Sudbury Street but on Court Street. Court Street and Sudbury Street run into each other, and Susan may well have not recognized or not remembered this fact.(31)]* In one room were wax figures, among them were the Simese twins that were connected by a band of flesh

Boston Museum. *Courtesy of the Society for the Preservation of New England Antiquities.*

about four inches wide that grew out of the side of each. Another groop was the trial of Christ by Pilot, large as life and dressed in oriental costumes and in charector. It was very impresive. While we were going through the rooms I heard the sweetest music I ever heard, and it was a mistery to me where it came from. At last I espied a high galery in one of the rooms and a band playing on stringed instruments, and I was charmed with the music. The Auditorium was very small as well as the stage, and the only performance was a dog dance and some songs.

My Aunt made me a new Cloak for winter. It was made long with sleves and cape and color [collar] [and] was belted around the waste with a cord and tassiles, which was a present from my young Uncle James. It was the fashion that winter to wear a long cord and tassle the colour of the cloak, mine was black but many of the girls wore them of different colours. They [the cloaks] [were] called Josies and were very warm and comfortable. The older women were [wore] short clocks [cloaks], pleated into a deep yoke and hung strate and plain to the kneens. The little girls were dressed very prettily in bright colours, trimed with swans down. I had a new bonnet of uncut velvet, trimed with french flowers.

I commenced school the first of Dec in an old school house on dearn St, where the resivour was afterwords built. *[The school Susan attended was known as the Bowdoin School, standing on the corner of Derne and Temple Streets. It was a school for girls after 1830, when the boys were transferred elsewhere. The school was destroyed in 1847 to build the Beacon Hill reservoir as part of the new water system (see above) and this reservoir, in turn, was removed about 1888.(32)]* It was two stories high and contained two large rooms on each floor. There were narrow winding stars that connected the two rooms [floors?]. In the morning we would study on the ground floor; in the afternoon we went up stares for our lessons. In one room they taught reading and grammar; geography and history in the other. They taught aritmatic and writeing so we had two setts of teachers. On one side of each room was a rased platform with three desks. The Master sat at the first one, and the Lady teachers sat at the other two: one in the midle and the other at the other end. And the school was devied into three devisons and each devision into three classes, so each teacher had her own diviesion and the Master superented the whole.

REMINISCENCE 61

First High School, corner of Derne and Temple Streets, Boston.
Courtesy of the Society for the Preservation of New England Antiquities.

Singing was introduced into the schools of Boston that year, and twice every week a singing Master would come in and drill the children in singing. His name was Lowell Mason, a composer and techer of music.

[Lowell Mason (1792-1872) is a recognized nineteenth-century American composer of church music and, additionally, is well regarded as a teacher of music. Susan was fortunate to be in Boston during the period he taught

in the public schools. He taught without pay in 1837, and then from 1838 to 1841 he received a salary. Susan is slightly in error, then, to report that 1841 was his first year of teaching. Mason once headed Boston's famous Handel and Haydn Society and was an early advocate of music conventions for training music instructors in the public schools.(33)]

In the rear of the school was a row of desks, where some of the oldest girls sat as Monitors to assist the teachers in watching and helping the small ones and reporting any misdemeaner to the Master.

I liked both my teachers very well. I never had any trouble but once, and that was in the writeing room with Master Robinson. He came along one day when I was writeing and grabed hold of my hand so rough that I was frightened and began to cry. His daughter, who was my teacher, told him to let me alone. He said, "She grips her pen!" She tried to console me [and] said he was very nervous and not to mind any thing about him. He was converet [converted] that winter under the preaching of Elder Knap and commenced haveing prayers in school. He had us all bow our heads down on our desks. But I dont remember much about his prayers, they were spoken so low. The other Masters name was Andrews. He had a kind and gentle disposition [and] was never severe in his punishments, but that was one of his duties. When the children were sent to him for that purpose, he would only give them three spanks on the hand. I never was punished so I dont know how much it hurt, but the little girls would go back to there seats crying.

[Susan recognized the value of Lowell Mason's teaching but seemed only partially to appreciate Robinson and Andrews. They were, however, very highly respected teachers. Abraham Andrews joined the Bowdoin School in 1822 and James Robinson began teaching there three

years later. They taught together for twenty-nine years at the Bowdoin School. Students remembered Andrews not being very severe just as Susan did, but they also recalled his excellent teaching of grammar. Robinson was best recalled for his teaching of penmanship, though Susan objected to his methods. Robinson's daughter was Mary S. Robinson who also taught at the school for many years, 1839-1862.(34)]

After school was dismissed in the afternoon, I would take long walks and so learned my way around the City. I would go up Washington St as far as dover St, which was the limit. It was terminated in a long road called the neck, which went to Roxbury through a saltmarsh which extended on both sides as far as the eye could see. The stores were very small, but I thought they were wanderfull. One window in a mileners store was my especial admireation. It had a wax figure in it as large as a child of five or six, dressed in the fashion of the day. I would stand and gaze at it as long as I had time. Sometimes I would go with some of the girls to the State house and climb the stares to the Cupelo and take a view of the City.

That winter there was a great revival in Boston led by Elder Knap. *["Elder Knap" was Elder Jacob Knapp, a well-known Baptist evangelic minister of the time. He arrived in Boston in December 1841 and stayed three months, preaching he tells us 180 sermons. He admitted to detesting Unitarians. Susan had read him quite correctly. His ministry in Boston was controversial and greatly affected the Boston scene, and threats of violence occurred. Rev. J. D. Fulton, then pastor of the Tremont Temple (Baptist), said of Knapp: "He fired no blank cartridges, but delivered broadsides at close range into the ranks of the foe."(35)]* He held meetings in all the Baptist Churches except one. Old Dr Sharp of Charles St would not admit him to his church and he was very wise, for some of the other churches were almost broken up by the class of people that were taken in at the time. He held the meetings all day, and every evening after the sermon he would have a testamony meeting. There would be no time lost but some one would be on there feet, speaking all the time. I remember one of his remarks as he was denouncing universalism: he said it was as imposible for a universalest to go to heaven as it was for a shad to climb an apple tree tail formost. As many of my best Friends were of that faith, I could not agree with him. He had nothing to say about the wanderfull love of Christ, but his sermons were full of threatnings and the torments of endless punishment. They had a new rivival hym book out called penroyal; the tunes were lively. *[It has been impossible to identify any hymnal of this period with such a title.]* And I liked the prayer meetings that were held in the church after he went away, for the singing was fine and took up most of the time.

My days were now full with going to school days and meetings at night. We went to Sunday School at half past nine then to church. After dinner we went to Sunday School at half past two, then another long sermon in the church in the afternoon, then the evening service. One evening we all went to a concert given by the school children in an old theater called the Odean. It was a very large building and had never been painted outside or in. And the Stage was very large with seats in the rear riseing one above another like an ampetheater, where all the singers sat; and there were hundreds of them, and there young voises sounded fine in the great building.

[The Odeon Theater was everything Susan recalled it as and much more. Odeon was a temporary name, the theater was usually known as the Federal Theater or the Boston Theater. It was located on Federal Street and was one of the best known architectural accomplishments of

REMINISCENCE 65

First Baptist Church, Boston. *Courtesy of the Society for the Preservation of New England Antiquities.*

Charles Bulfinch, who designed it as Boston's first theater. It was torn down in 1852. At the time of Susan's visit, the theater was in one of its periods of decline and dramas were no longer being performed there. It had been leased for a long time to the Boston Academy of Music. The theater had seats for fifteen hundred people and had been elaborately decorated. Susan remembered it as unpainted, but it had been renovated in the late 1830s and painted inside.(36)]

One day a Lady called and invited me to go to Malbourgh Chapel to see some Mendian Africans who were to be on exibition that afternoon. They had been kidnaped on the Coast of Africa and put into the hold of a slave ship and were on there way to the Southern States to be sold in the slave market, when they revolted and killed the Captain and crew and took command of the ship. And [they] were trying to navigate her, when they were found by a passing ship and brought to Boston and put in jail. Some missionaries took them in charge, learned them to read and speak the inglish language and were going to send them back to Africa as teachers. There were a number of young men and a girl fourteen and a small Boy, who was the Son of a king. He could talk very good inglish. He said he was down on the beach playing when a Man came and catched him and put him in a hole. One of the Men made a speach in his native tongue and another told in inglish of there treatment on board the vesel. They were told they were going to be killed and packed in a barrel and salted. He made all the motions as he told the story of what they were going to do to him. The girl read the fourteenth Chapter of John. They were all as black as the ace of spades and they sailed [for] Africa.

[It is fitting that Susan recalled this scene in some detail, for she was witnessing the finale of a rather famous and strange affair. She had some details incorrect, either from a faulty memory or from misinformation learned at the time, and she would probably have been appalled had she known all the facts. These Mendian blacks (Mendian is an African dialect spoken in Sierra Leone) had in fact rebelled against their Spanish

slavers. The story of their being threatened with the boiling pot ironically came from a black cook on the slave ship. After capturing their ship they landed off Long Island, where they were apprehended by authorities and first imprisoned at New London and then tried as escaped slaves at New Haven. The plight of the blacks attracted the interest of the Abolitionists. Since the blacks were claimed as slaves by Spain, President van Buren's government took the attitude that the courts really should not try the escaped men but should turn them over to Spain. The government was convinced that the trial, however, would go against the blacks and kept a ship in the harbor to spirit them away before any appeal could be made. The judge, to the government's surprise, ruled in favor of the blacks, and it was the government which appealed the decision to the Supreme Court. There, John Quincy Adams argued the case for the blacks and won. As Susan indicated, the blacks were then educated as missionaries who hoped they would carry the Christian faith to their people when returned to their Mendi tribesmen. They were only partially successful in this, but the societies organized to aid these blacks merged to form the American Missionary Association.(37)]

One afternoon my Uncle took the two little Boys and my self out on the Common to see the muster. All the milertaruy compays in the state were called out for there anuel muster. They made quite a big display, but when they began to fire cannons we wanted to go home. The boys were frightened. There Father had taken us up so close that the noise was something awfull, and we beged to go home. But there was a great Croud and tables were spread on the side walk on beacon St, an they all seemed to be haveing a good time. But I was glad to get home out of the noise.

There was no school on wednesday and Saturday afternoons. Sometimes I would manage to be late in the morning, when the doors would be locked, and there would be no admitance; and I would have a day off. The next morning I would have to cary a writen excuse for absence.

One morning my Aunt and I went to a long walk to Watertown, and I injoyed it very much. We went through Old Cambridge past Longfellows residence and a number of fine old places. We had a very plesent visit with my Aunt. After dinner she took us out for a drive. We went to one of the show places of the town. The grounds were quite extensive and the house was some distance from the St. There were three long avnues that led to the house, bordered with shade threes through a well kept lawn. At the prenciple entrance was a pretty little Cottage where the gate keeper lived with his family. The house was very large and plane looking. In the rear was a very large garden with flowers of every discription, inclosed with a high brick wall. Near the top of the wall was an insertion of China made in a kind of greacian patern and toped off with a row of pressed brick. He had fruit trees trained against the wall like vines with the branches growing out strait on bith sides, that were bearing pears of a large size. He had green houses with tropical plants and grape vines that bore grapes in winter. We went into a house wher a woman lived who did nothing but washing for the family. He [the owner] had a hundred shirts that were kept in two piles, and he was so affraid of getting a damp shirt that he would go through the hundred shirts before he would commence on the fresh pile. He was very excentric and his children were not aloud to assoiate with other children but had a tutor, who would take them out in a carrage or on horse back. When he died the place was cut up into house lots and sold, and the children went to Boston to live.

I[n] Jan 1842 they wrote us from home of the death of Grand Father Patten. Soon after, Uncle James went to Manchester and stayed a week at my Fathers. When he came back he told me mother had had a very hard time, and he did not see how she had ever lived through it all. The day Grand Father was burried my little Sister was not expected to live through the day. After the railroad men went away the small children were taken sick with scarlet fever; and it had been so fatal among Children in the city, she was affraid to have the Dr. So she took care of them herself. After they all got well, the Dr called one day as he was going by and told her she had done well. But he had burried seven little children—all he ever had. *[All efforts to confirm such a scarlet fever epidemic in Manchester at this time failed.]*

In Feb I received a letter from my Sister with the request that I send a name for another little Sister who had just arived upon the stage of life. I wrote that I thought Josephine Lazett would be a pretty name. She wrote they had named her Mary Josephine; they all thought Lazett was two frenchefied.

I was now very uneasy and anxious to go home; but they thought I had better stay until June, for my Aunt wanted to do some sewing for me before I went. And she wanted me to keep house for her, while she went on a viset to NH, for Uncle James and a Lady who had two rooms in the house and had her meals with us.

She [the lady lodger] carried on a large milenary estabelishment on Washington St and imployed a number of girls. At that time they used very fine straw for bonnets called the florence braid. It was very expensive but could be sewed over a number of times and pressed into shape again. There were cheaper braids called the dunstable and leghorn. She made a great deal of money. She would sometimes invite me to go out with her and liked to have me come to the store for a change.

One day while on my way to the store, I met a very tall, strange looking Man without a nose. He looked so singuler that I inquired about him of my Friend. She said he was a very rich Man without wif or Family and boarded in one of the Hotels and always [took] his meals in his room. Once he offered any Lady in Boston a thousand dollers to walk the length of washington St with him, but no one would except the offer.

A few years after, my Friend married a young Man of twenty four. She was twice his age. She retirid from business, bought a fine place in Roxbury, and set her husband up in business. But he failed and lost a lot of money, and she became insane and died in a lunitic Asylum in two weeks.

The family [her aunt] came home from NH, and I was more anxious than ever to go home and help my Mother. So, on the first of June, I bid good by to Boston and all my friends and started for Manchester. I came in sight of the new school house just as it was closing for the afternoon. My Sister came runing to meet me and I met her half way and clasped her in my arms and lifted her off the ground, for I had grown large and strong while she was small and delicate looking. My little Sister was there and I was glad to be at home. When we got to the house, Mother stood in the door with the baby in her arms and was just as proud of her as though she had been the first and only one. She had great black eyes and a lot of dark brown hair and was four months old.

All the Children seemed glad to see me, and when my baggage came I gave them the little presents I had brought for them. Uncle James sent the baby a pink french calico dress; it was fifty cents a yard and was very becoming to her when she was old enough to wear it. The other little ones had little painted pails full of candy. I was so excited and glad to see them all that I ran all over the place. One of the girls came after me to go after the cows as I had been in the habit of doing before I went away, and it seemed so good to go through the woods again after being shut up in the City so long. My sister and I that evening sang all the songs in my school book and penroyal himn book. She loved to sing and had a very sweet voice. Father would often ask her to sing for him, and I could sing better with her than I could alone.

I was glad to be at home and able to help Mother, and I took it upon myself to do the heavest part of the work. She went away visiting this summer and had a good long rest while we kept house.

The cars [railroad] commenced runing about this time and was a great curiosity to all of us. We would all start and run as soon as we saw them comeing and would stand and gaze at them open mouthed to see them go past. There were never more than two pasenger and one baggage car on a train, and there were only two trains a day at first. One went in the morning at eight for Boston and another from Boston at four in the afternoon.

The Boys owned a large dog that they had raised from a puppy and were very fond of him. When he saw the cars comeing he would give chase and try to outrun them. The Engineneer and fire man would strike on the outside of the Tender with peices of flat board and try to inrage him, and one day he got a head of the engine and was run over and was killed. The Boys blamed the men for the death of there dog. He used to set and sing when he heard the clanging of the heavy facktory bells; he would

Granite bridge, built in 1840—Concord Railroad, opened in 1842. *From the Manchester Historic Association Photo Archives.*

point his nose up in the air and make a funny noise, something betwene a bark and yelp.

The Boys missed there old playmate and made there plans to get even with the men and have some fun at there expence. So the first day of April they dressed up a scare crow, put a big red cabbage on for a head with a tall hat on and, very early in the morning, layed it acrost the track. When the morning train came along the Men saw it and blew there whistles and rang there bell but ran over it before they [could] stop the train. Then they looked back and were horrow stricken to see blood all over the track, but when they reached the Man they found red cabage cut up and strewed all over the track. The Boys were hiden where they could see all that was going on but no one out of the family ever knew who put it there. There was quite a peice in the newspaper about it. They called it a good April fool Joke, and the Boys thought they had a little satisfaction for the death of there dog.

[This story of Susan's brothers retaliating against the railroad men for the death of their dog made the local newspaper as Susan noted, but its full meaning is found only in Susan's memoir. The newspaper story was carried under a headline of "Clear the Track! The Best of the Season." The report, whose headline revealed due credit, followed: "On Saturday last, as the upward train of cars, filled with passengers, was progressing under full steam-pressure, about three miles below this place, where there was a turn in the road, a man was suddenly discovered, a few rods ahead, lying directly across the track. The whistle was immediately made to screech in its wildest strains and every means taken to haul up; but all the exertions were unavailing. The train had passed several rods too far, and the conductors and others jumped through the cars to the rear end, shouting 'a man

Amoskeag machine shop ca. 1850. *From the Manchester Historic Association Photo Archives.*

run over'—Horror dwelt on every countenance; the paleness of death itself was on every cheek! Long and hasty strides soon brought the company around the mangled 'man' who laid with his head one side of the track and body the other, completely severed, while were streaming from both head and shoulders (BIG WISPS OF STRAW!) The body was tossed high in the air, with exclamations, 'd—dly fooled!' Reader' it was the FIRST DAY OF APRIL." (38)]

One day an old Man who had been drinking hard came walking down the tracts from the city. When it was time for the four oclock train, he paid no attention to the tooting of the whistle or the bell ringing. So they stoped the train and pulled him out of danger. He said he was not going to be driven out of the road by there old cooking stove.

There were now two more large Cotton Mills in opperation called the Amosnoskeag Co. The first one was called the Starck Co. The first Baptist and the free will Bapist Churches were built while I was gone. *[The Amoskeag Company encouraged the establishment of churches in Manchester as an integral part of its planning of the city. Lots were early set aside for churches, and deeds were made available for this land over a period of many decades. Susan remembered accurately the first churches awarded lots. Sometimes the land was assigned many months ahead of the deed being awarded, but between 1839 and 1842, when Susan returned from Boston, the First Congregational, First Universalist, First Baptist, Free Will Baptist, and Second Methodist had all received allocations of land. Eventually the awarding of land to churches was extended to the Catholic church, including various ethnic denominations. The French Catholics were first awarded land in 1880, when the*

French Canadians began to emerge as the single largest ethnic group among the employees of the mills.(39)] The Methodest and univerlatest churches were first pland as well as the Cong[regational] and the Episcopal Churches. In the center of the town was a very old Methodest Church where we went with the rest of the young folks. The principle St in the new part of the town was named Elm St. It ran parelell with the river at a distance of about one fourth of a mile and was a business Street and had stores on both sides. The land on the west was reserved for the use of the coperation [corporation] and [the city] was laid out very reguler with little parks every few blocks. The boarding houses were built of brick, very uniform in appearence. On the east side [of Elm St.] were residencial streets that extended back to the hills in the distance like an inclined plane. The site for the City was beautifully situated like a great level plane riseing gradualy to the hills beyond.

 A number of the young girls my age and many that were much older worked in the Mills. There were no foreigners imployed then, but the operatives were all from Country towns in Vermont and NH and many came from the Cotten Mills in Mass. *[The labor force in Manchester drew heavily on local girls for its early operatives, and the management of Amoskeag assumed a paternalistic responsibility for the moral well-being of the young women. This labor force was altered radically as more men were employed and as foreign workers were recruited. But the management not only continued its paternalism long after such ideals waned in the sister mill communities but refined and updated its approach in the twentieth century, probably making the Manchester mill scene unique.(40)]* Many of the small Farmers, who had more Children than money, sold there farms and moved to Manchester where they could all work in the Mill. They made good wages and worked long hours. The work started at five in the morning the year round. At seven they had a half hour for breakfast and another half hour at noon for dinner and worked until seven at night. Some of the girls were ambitious for an education and would save up there money and go away to some school. Some would help support a Brother through Collage. One of our neighbors girls was very fond of music, and she bought herself a Peano and paid for music lessons and became a fine singer and Peanoest. At one time the girls published a magazine called *the offering.*

[Apparently Susan is here confused. She may have been referring to a well-known paper published in Lowell called the Offering *and edited by women. Or she might have been recalling a short-lived publication of Manchester and Lowell called the* Manchester Operative. *But this paper was not published by mill girls, despite one being pictured on the masthead, and it was not published until 30 December 1843.(41)]*

Most of the girls that I was acquainted with worked in the Spining room where there were hundreds of young girls worked. Some of them not more than nine or ten years old. They were called doffers because there work was to take off the full bobbins and put on empty ones. It was not very hard work and they had long resting spells betwene, while the bobbins were being filled. But the long hours of confinement was very hard on them. After a few years they were obliged to go to school six months out of the year, and could not go to work unless they brought a cirtificate that they had been to school the required time. The weavers and dressers made the best wages. They could earn two dollars a day besides there board, if they were quick and strong.

Susan Baker Blunt at age thirty. *From the Manchester Historic Association Photo Archives.*

They were all paid off on the same day and then there would be such a rush at the stores. There were only two or three dry goods stores in the town then, and they were mostly dependent on the factory girls trade. One night one of the girls wanted to buy some pink calico for a dress. There was none in the store, so the store keeper cut off a blue one and handed her the package. She said, "I oredered pink." He said, "You can imagine this is pink and it will do as well." She went out with the dress, and he followed her to the door and demanded his money. She told him to imagine it was paid for and it would do as well and went off with the dress.

In the fall my sister went to school in Piscataquoque and boarded at home. She had to walk a mile and a half, but in bad weather the Boys carried her over. She injoyed the school very much and that winter went to Boston to stay a while with my Aunt where I had spent the year before. I attended the winter and summer district schools until I was eighteen.

And in May fifteenth 1843, I celibrated my fifteenth birth day by getting up at one oclock in the morning and doing a large washing and then going with some of the girls to the City to see the sights, as I was now a young woman and done with childish things. I will close this simple naritive hopeing it be of some interest to my Friends.

Susan S Blunt

Appendix

1. Sophronia — born 1822
2. Willard — born 1824
3. Dewitt Clinton — born 1826
4. Susan — born 1828
5. James Thornton — born 1832
6. George W. — born 1835
7. Robert Bradford — born 1837
8. Margaret — born 1839
9. Mary Josephine — born 1842
10. Frances Effie — born 1845
11. Elbridge — born 1847
12. Solon — born 1850

Bibliographic References

1. Joseph F. Kett, *Rites of Passage* (New York, 1977), 98. For comments on colonial demography see especially Philip J. Greven, Jr., *Four Generations: Population, Land, and Family in Colonial Andover, Massachusetts* (Ithaca and London, 1970) and Kenneth A. Lockridge, "The Population of Dedham, Massachusetts, 1636-1736," *English Historical Review* 19 (1966): 318-44.

2. See B.A. Botkin, ed., *A Treasury of New England Folklore* (revised ed., New York, 1935), 418-22.

3. Hobart Pillsbury, *New Hampshire: Resources, Attractions, and Its People. A History* (4 vols., New York, 1927), vol. 2, 398, and Donald B. Cole, *Jacksonian Democracy in New Hampshire, 1800-1851* (Cambridge, MA, 1970), 160-61.

4. George Waldo Browne, *The Amoskeag Manufacturing Co. of Manchester, New Hampshire: A History* (Manchester, NH, 1915), 121.

5. *The Militia Law of New Hampshire, to which are annexed Orders of the Commander-in-chief, with the Adjutant General's Instructions and the Forms and Course of Inspection and Review* (Concord, NH, 1843), 57, 59-60.

6. See "Census of Hillsborough County, 1820," made by John Secombe, Assistant to the Marshal of the District of New Hampshire. [Handwritten] Collection of New Hampshire Historical Society, Concord.

7. Daniel Creamer and Charles W. Coulter, *Labor and the Shutdown of the Amoskeag Textile Mills* (Philadelphia: Projects Administration National Research Project No. L-5, 1939), 148, 155.

8. For a sane but old coverage of the burning of the Charlestown convent, see James Phinney Munroe, *The New England Conscience* (Boston, 1915), 117-39.

9. See especially Barbara Finkelstein, "Pedagogy as Intrusion: Teaching Values in Popular Primary Schools in Nineteenth Century America," *History of Childhood Quarterly: The Journal of Psychohistory* 2 (Winter 1975): 355-60. For some examples of New Hampshire school discipline see Pillsbury, *New Hampshire,* vol. 4, 993-95.

10. C.T. Adam, *The Family of James Thornton* (New York, 1905), 8.

11. See Will W. Tracy, *Tomato Culture* (New York, 1918), 14-19.

12. See "Matches," *Encyclopedia Americana* (New York, 1972), vol. 18, 422a-23.

13. Manchester Town Book, 414. [Handwritten] Collection of Manchester Historic Association.

14. Letter. Hazel Kimball to Elizabeth Lessard, librarian of Manchester Historic Association, 29 June 1969. Susan Blunt file.

15. Pillsbury, *New Hampshire,* vol. 4, 969.

16. See Manfred Bachman and Claus Hansmann, *Dolls the Wide World Over* (New York, 1973), 122, and Dorothy S., Elizabeth A., and Evelyn J. Coleman, *The Collector's Encyclopedia of Dolls* (New York, 1968), 18, 638.

17. Jane Shadel Spillman, "Cup Plates in America," *Antiques* 104 (August 1973): 216-19.

18. See Howard Parker Moore, *The Patten Families: Genealogies of the Pattens* (Ann Arbor, MI, 1939), 24. Moore's work does have, however, some typographical errors and must not be taken as definitive.

19. See reports of the School Committee in "Annual Reports" for the Town of Manchester, 1844-1845 and 1845-1846, and for the City of Manchester, 1850, 1852, 1853, 1854, 1863, and 1864. Also see School Committee Minutes, City of Manchester, 2 September 1881 and 7 October 1881, vol. "C" and 7 December 1883, vol. "D." [Handwritten] Manchester School Department.

20. See *History of Bedford New Hampshire from 1737* (Concord, 1903), 1039. Moore's genealogical study of the Pattens noted that Polly "had a fine memory." Moore, *The Patten Families,* 24.

21. Browne, *The Amoskeag Manufacturing Co.,* 62-63. Some people credit Ezekiel Straw, early associated with the Amoskeag management, with making the basic plan for the central city. See Grace Holbrook Blood, *Manchester on the Merrimack* (Manchester, NH, 1975 [1948]), 109-110.

22. John C. Gunn, *Gunn's New Family Physician or Home Book of Health forming a complete household guide* (Cincinnati, 1870), 768.

23. Ira Warren, *Household Physician for the use of Families, Planters, Seamen, and Travellers* (Boston, 1864), 435-36.

24. Moore, *The Patten Families,* 24.

25. *King's Handbook of Boston* (Cambridge, MA, 1878), 74.

26. Samuel Adam Drake, *A Book of New England Legends and Folk Lore* (Boston, 1910), 35.

27. Justin Winsor, ed., *The Memorial History of Boston 1630-1880* (4 vols., Boston, 1881), vol. 2, 90-91; *King's Handbook of Boston,* 22; and the *Boston Directory* (Boston, 1841), for the house number for Phineas Blunt, who was listed as a soapstoneworker.

28. For a brief but satisfactory account of the history of the construction of this monument, giving costs and fund drives, see Richard Frothingham, *History of the Siege of Boston, and of the Battles of Lexington, Concord, and Bunker Hill* (New York, 1970 [1903]), 337-59.

29. Moore, *The Patten Families,* 24.

30. M. A. DeWolfe Howe, *Boston Landmarks* (New York, 1946), 101.

31. See Abel Bowen, *Bowen's Picture of Boston or the Citizen's and Stranger's Guide to the Metropolis of Massachusetts and its environs* (Boston, 1838), 200.

32. Leah H. Nichols-Wellington, *History of the Bowdoin School, 1812-1907* (Manchester, NH, 1912).

33. Frederick H. Martens, "Lowell Mason," *Dictionary of American Biography,* vol. 11, 371-72.

34. Nichols-Wellington, *History of the Bowdoin School,* 6, 12-13, 27, 121-24.

35. See Jacob Knapp, *Autobiography of Elder Jacob Knapp.* Introductory essay by R. Jeffrey (New York, 1868), 124-25. Fulton's quote, 134.

36. Perhaps the best description of this significant building is to be found in Harold and James Kirker's *Bulfinch's Boston 1787-1817* (New York, 1964), 59-63. Also see Bowen, *Bowen's Picture of Boston,* 71-73, and William W. Clapp, Jr., *A Record of the Boston Stage* (Boston, 1853), 67-68.

37. For an excellent account of this episode see Fred J. Cook, "The Slave Ship Rebellion," *American Heritage* 8 (February 1957): 60-64, 104-106.

38. *The Manchester Democrat,* 5 April 1843, 2.

39. See Browne, *The Amoskeag Manufacturing Co.*, 122-24.

40. See Particularly Tamara K. Hareven, "The Laborers of Manchester, New Hampshire, 1912-1922: The Role of Family and Ethnicity in Adjustment to Industrial Life," *Labor History* 16 (Spring 1975): 250-51. Also see Hareven, "Family Time and Industrial Time: Family and Work in a Planned Corporation Town, 1900-1914," *Journal of Urban History* 1 (May 1975): 365-89.

41. See Howard A. Chamberlen, *The First Ten Years of Printing and Publishing in Manchester, N.H., 1839-1849: A Preliminary Survey* (Manchester, NH, 1948), 13.

Index

[n = Editor's italicized note]

Adams, John Quincy, 67n
Adams, Thomas (Susan Baker's first husband), 11n
American Missionary Association, 67n
Amoskeag Manufacturing Company, 47, 47n, 75-77
Andrews, Master Abraham (teacher), 62, 62n
Anti-Catholicism in Boston, 29n
April Fool joke by Baker boys on railroad men, 73-74
Astral lamp, 35, 35n
Aunt Jenny, 25-26, 26n

Baker family: Dewitt Clinton (brother), 26, 27, 38, 44; Elbridge (brother), 9n, 15; Frances Effie (sister), 35n; George W. (brother), 23, 40; Grandfather, 42, 44; James Thornton (brother), 18, 23; Margaret (sister), 42, 70, 79; Margaret Patten (mother), 15n, 18-24, 32-33, 37, 39-40, 43-45, 49, 53, 70, 71; Mary Josephine (sister), 69-71; Robert (father), 15n, 16, 18, 20, 22-23, 28-31, 38, 44-45, 45n, 49, 53; Robert Bradford aka "Capt. Bob" (brother), 38, 40, 44, 52-53; Solon (youngest brother), 80; Sophronia (sister), 19, 27, 31, 39-40, 42, 43n, 44, 45n, 46-47,, 49, 53, 69, 70-71; Susan, 7-13n and photos 14, 78; Willard (brother), 27, 30-31, 40, 42, 44. Also see Appendix.
Bakersville School, 44-45, 45n
Bedford, 46n
Blacks in Merrimack, 26n
Blacksmith Robert Baker, 16, 22, 26, 28
Blunt, Phineas (Susan Baker's second husband), 11n
Boarding houses, 16, 47n, 53
Boatmen, 16-17, 21
Boston and environs observed: Baptist Sunday School, 64; Beacon Street, 67; Bowdoin School, 60-63; Bunker Hill and Monument, 57; Cambridge, 68; Charles Street Baptist Church, 63; Charlestown, 29; [Boston] Common, 54-55, 57, 67; Derne Street, 60; Dover Street, 63; Faneuil Hall, 58; frog pond, 55; Longfellow's residence, 68; Lyceum Lectures, 58;

85

Marlborough Chapel, 66; the [Boston] Museum, 58-59; Odeon Theater, 64; Old South Church, 55; Province House and Court, 55; Public Garden, 55; Quincy Markets, 58; Roxbury, 63, 70; State House, 63; Universalism, 64; Washington Street, 55, 70; Watertown garden estate and outbuildings, 68-69
Brackish drinking water in Boston, 58
Brick oven, 57
Bulfinch, Charles, 65n

Canals, 16, 28, 47
Candle dipping with children's help, 35
Child molester. See Man in cemetery
Churches (Manchester): Catholic, 75-76n; Episcopal, 76; First Baptist, 75, 75n; First Congregational, 75n, 76; First Free Will Baptist, 75, 75n; First Universalist, 75n, 76; Second Methodist, 75n, 76
Cicero Sweat household, 26n
Circus: travelling, 21; children's, 27
Clothing: "Josie" cloak, 60; Mary Josephine's pink French calico baby dress, 71; mill girl's dress fabric, 79; straw braid for bonnets, 69-70; Susan's 9-pence calico apron, 42; white party dresses, 39-40
Concord, N.H., 20, 21n, 36n
Cooking stove; the first in Merrimack, 33
Coolidge, A. (first husband of Hannah Patten), 57n
Cranberrying, 40
Cup plates, 41, 41n

Dancing, 24
Deavall, John (second husband of Hannah Patten), 57n
Deputy Sheriff Robert Baker, 38, 44
Doctors' visits, 37, 38, 44, 50, 52-53, 69
Doffers, 77
Dolls: ragbabies, 27, 38; wax, 38
Dressers, 77

Elder Knap [Elder Jacob Knapp], 63

Fireplace (for cooking), 33, 42
Fishing at Amoskeag Falls, 21-22
Food, eating and preparing: apples, 33-34; biscuits and honey, 41; boiled dinner, 26; Boston food, 57, 58; bread and butter, 18-19; Bunker Hill Day feast, 24; cup custard, 23; doughnuts, 37; farm breakfast, 42; Fourth of July feast, 24; party food, 51; tomatoes, 32-33, 32-33n; turtle, 27
Fool Peabody, 25
French Canadians, 75-76n

Hillsborough County, 16
Horseshoe Pond (Merrimack), 26-27

Illnesses and remedies: brain fever, 44; [the common] cold, 41; scalding, 49-50, 50n; scarlet fever, 69; whooping cough, 52
Indians. See Penobscot Indians at Thornton's Ferry
Irish immigrants: Baker's encounter with, 28-29; presence in Manchester labor force, 28n

Jeneral Jackson [President Andrew Jackson], 20-21, 20-21n

INDEX

Kimball, Hazel (great-niece), 35n
Kitchen utensils, 33
Knifebox fashioned by Dewitt Clinton Baker, 27

Lake Winepasawque [Winnipesaukee], 21
Lamprey eels, 21
Lawrence dam, 22
Lawyers, 16, 42-43
Lowell, 21n, 28
Lunatics, 25, 36-37

Man in cemetery, 49
Manchester Operative, 77n
Mason, Lowell (singing master), 61, 61-62n
Matches: home manufacture, 34; friction matches, 34n
Mendian Africans, 66-67
Mental illness, 36n
Merrimack River, 16, 18, 21, 22, 24
Merrimack (town), 16, 21n
Military displays: May training, 25; muster on Boston Common, 67
Mill employees: builders, 28, 28n; girls, 76-79; hands, 76n
Milliner friend, 69-70
Montreal, 29

Nashua, 53, 54
New babies in Baker home, 1832-1842: James Thornton, 18; George W., 23; Robert Bradford, 39; Margaret, 42; Mary Josephine, 69
Nuns; Father's generosity toward travellers in need, 29

The Offering, 77, 77n
Orphan cousin's visit, 39-40

Parlor games: blind man's bluff, 49-50; looking glass futures, 51

Patten family: Alexander (grandfather), 43, 43n, 69; David (uncle and twin of Isaac), 43n; Grandmother, 43, 44, 46; Greenleaf (uncle), 43n; Hannah (aunt), 57n; Isaac (uncle and twin of David), 43n; James (uncle), 43n, 58, 69, 71; Jean (great-aunt), 46n; John (uncle), 43n; Mary (great-Aunt Polly), 46; Matthew (great-grandfather), 15n, 43n; Sally Hutchinson (wife of John Patten), 43n; Sarah (great-aunt), 46; Susannah (aunt of Susan, wife of Phineas Blunt), 54, 54n, 60, 68, 69
Penobscot Indians at Thornton's Ferry, 22
Pets: calf, 27; dog, 71-75; raccoon, 23
Pewter platters, 26
Pine grove and springs near Manchester home, 51-52
Piscataquog School, 79
Playing ball with turtle eggs, 27
Pudding stick fashioned from shingle by Willard Baker, 27

Quebec, 28

Railroad: Nashua to Concord construction, 53; Nashua to Boston trip in steam cars, 54
Rivermen, 16-17
Robinson, Mary S. (teacher), 62, 63n
Robinson, Master James (teacher), 62, 62-63n

Sand as woodwork cleaner, 26
School, 18, 20, 30-31, 44-45, 45n, 58, 60-63, 68
Shad salmon, 21
Shopkeepers, 16, 18, 79
Singing at home, 51, 71

Singing School, 39-40, 61-62
Sleigh riding, 24
"Smoking out teacher," 30
So Ever Club, 9n
Stage to Nashua, 54
Starck Company [Stark Manufacturing Company], 75
Suncook, NH, 50-51n
Swift's pasture near Manchester home, 52

Taverns, 16, 21, 29, 35; Colonial architecture of, 23-24
Teamsters, 16
Thanksgiving, 19-20

Thornton, Senator James Bounaparte, 32, 32n
Thornton's Ferry, 16
Tomato, uses of, 32

Ursuline nuns. See Nuns; Father's generosity toward

van Buren, Martin, 21n, 67n
Vermont, 16

Washington, D.C., 32, 35
Weavers, 34, 77
West Covina, California, 13n
Whale oil illumination, 35
Woodstove (for heating), 57